Make a list of your favourite content, so you know which pages to go back to exam!

Dominic Salles still lives in Swindon, with his workaholic wife Deirdre, his jiu-jitsu-loving engineer son, Harry, and Bob, the 15 year old rescue dog who refuses to die. His sister Jacey is world famous for her Spanish accent. She would be hilarious in her own YouTube channel. His daughter Jess has just become a teacher and coach to the Welsh women's Aussie Rules Football team. He drives a 2006 Prius.

His YouTube channel, Mr Salles Teaches English, will one day earn him a living. When that happens, he is going to train as a snowboard instructor, in January 2021

He has just bought a longboard and is building thighs like The Rock because, you know, it will happen!

How to Use This Guide

Welcome to a **world first!** This is the first guide integrated with video and designed around the principles of cognitive science: retrieval practice, spaced learning, interleaving, elaboration, and dual coding.

For several years I've been showing teachers and their students how to get grades 7, 8 and 9 with my guides and YouTube videos. An astonishing 27% of viewers report going up 3 or more grades from their mocks after using my videos.

But what if I could double that, so that 50% of students who bought my guide got **Grade 7** or more? What does such a guide look like? It looks like this. For a start, it includes 19 Grade 9 essays!

7 Ways You Will Get Top Grades

1. **Retrieval Practice**.

   a) That means you would see me teach a *scene* once in a video, while you take notes next to the key quotations in the guide.
   b) The second retrieval practice is reading the guide.
   c) For the third retrieval, I include some short activities to help you get the ideas into your own words.
   d) The fourth is at the end of each Act, when you summarise the most important quotations and ideas you want to remember from that Act.
   e) The fifth is the end of the guide, where you have note taking sheets for the key quotations for each **character** and **theme** for the whole play.

Because you have to think about what you have learned 5 times it will simply stay in your memory. The exam will need no thinking time – boom, ideas will pop out onto your page.

2. **Spaced Practice.** Don't tackle all the activities above at once. Space them out over time. It will just make you remember more, **because** your brain works that way.

3. **Elaboration**. The pictures you draw, and the boxed activities all help you find ways to make sense of the information you've read, and find different ways to make it memorable.

4. **Dual Coding**. The pictures you draw build connections in your memory, so remembering what you need in the exam is easy. Being taught twice, once in video form, and once in writing, also helps you get the information in dual ways.

5. **Explaining the Steps**. When you read, you can see how the ideas build from **Grade 6** to grades 9 and beyond. You can choose to read the guide page by page, or you can read it the first time just reading the **Grade 6** paragraphs, the second time just reading **Grade 7**, and so on.

6. **Model Essays**. Each analysis of the *scene* builds to write an essay which will help you write about the extract, link to other parts of the play, link to **context** and to **Shakespeare**'s purpose. Each one is an essay that will get you 100% in the exam.

7. **Interleaving**. You are probably studying something different in class. If your teacher is using this book and my videos, they should mix things up, so you aren't studying Macbeth every lesson. Mixing what you study in this way feels weird, but builds stronger memories.

What Gets You the Grades?

Grade 6

The 2019 Grade Boundaries for AQA were 98 out of 160 for a **Grade 6** . This is 61.25%. Let's call it 62%.This is 18.6 marks out of 30 on the **Shakespeare** question. Let's call it 19.

The skills for 19 out of 30 are:

AO1

Clear and explained, but not yet thoughtful and developed.

With effective quotations, but not yet integrated or embedded into your **interpretation** or **interpretation**s. (In other words, at **Grade 6** they are still written as PEE paragraphs).

AO2

Clear explanation of Shakespeare's methods, and how this affects the audience, but not yet examining how this affects the **audience**'s **interpretation**s of **characters** or **themes**. To examine you would have to consider more than one **interpretation**.

Appropriate use of relevant subject terminology, but not yet using subject terminology effectively (for example, naming it, but not saying why it is important).

AO3

Clear understanding of ideas, or perspectives, or contextual factors which would have affected the audience of the time (*Jacobean* **in the case of Macbeth).** But not yet making detailed links with more than one **interpretation**.

So, as you can see, **Grade 6** is not so hard. You just have to make sure you get the basics right, *all the way through your essay.*

The basics are:

1. Write a clear point of **view** about the question as your thesis.
2. Know the right quotations to back up your arguments.
3. Write about **context**, and link it to your **interpretation**.
4. Explain what methods **Shakespeare** is using, and how that would have made **readers** of the time think about the **character** or **theme**.
5. Use the right subject terminology, without mistakes.

Grades 8 and 9

In the top band, where grades 8 and 9 are hiding, you need:

AO1

Critical, exploratory, conceptualised response to task and whole text. This simply means writing about the whole play, especially the ending where **characters** and **themes** are resolved. The ending is where we can work out **Shakespeare**'s intentions.

To be exploratory you need to write about more than one **interpretation**. To be conceptualised you must show why one way of **interpret**ing **Shakespeare**'s purpose is better than another.

Judicious use of precise references to support interpretation(s). Pick the right quotations. Job done in this guide!

AO2

Analysis of writer's methods with subject terminology used judiciously. All the analysis shows you what the right terminology is.

Exploration of effects of writer's methods on reader. This is easy – every time you write about **Shakespeare**'s purpose, you cover the effect he wants to have on the **reader**.

AO3

Exploration of ideas/perspectives/contextual factors. Again, having more than one **interpretation** and linking to **Shakespeare**'s purpose always does this.

Shown by specific, detailed links between context/text/task. Linking the **context** to **Shakespeare**'s purpose always pushes you towards the top grades.

So, what do you really have to do?

1. Write about **Shakespeare**'s purposes.

2. Have more than one way of looking at these. This is so easy for Macbeth, **because** one **audience** is the king, who wants to be flattered, another is the nobles who might want to remove or assassinate him, and another is the king who **Shakespeare** wants to influence. And then obviously, it is written for the paying public who want to be entertained. The marks just give themselves away!

3. Discuss the **context** when dealing with each purpose.

4. Base everything you write on quotations.

5. The only hard bit – be detailed – write 700 -1000 words. When you get to the end of the guide you will know so much, that target will be easy, as you genuinely will not have to think.

What are the 3 main ideas you want to remember so far?

1._____

_____

2._____

_____

3._____

_____

A Note on Iambic Pentameter

Knowing this will help you write brilliantly about Shakespeare's purpose and effect on the reader.

Shakespeare gives his lines ten **syllables**. Each **syllable** is paired with another. In the **iambic** form, the first **syllable** is not **emphasise**d, but the second is. These two **syllables** are called a foot. So, it is 'pentameter' **because** it has five (pent = five in Ancient **Greek**) feet. And as each foot has two **syllables**, pentameter has ten **syllables**.

Ok, so what?

> "The **Prince** of **Cum**ber**land**! That **is** a **step**
>
> On **which** I **must** fall **down**, or **else** o'er**leap**,
>
> For **in** my **way** it **lies**. Stars, **hide** your **fires**;
>
> Let **not** light **see** my **black** and **deep** des**ires**".

Shakespeare used it to show his actors how to deliver the lines, letting them know which parts of words to **emphasise**. He also only gives **iambic pentameter** to his **characters** of noble birth.

Some people believe it recreates the heartbeat, **because** is goes te – TUM – te – TUM – te – TUM – te TUM – te – Tum, which is the same sort of logic that says you use a comma when you pause. Maybe, but you use most punctuation where you could pause, especially full stops.

With **meter**, it's similar. For example, this would also sound like a heartbeat: TUM – te – TUM – te – TUM – te – TUM – te – Tum – te – . This **meter** is called **trochaic**, where the **emphasis** comes on the first **syllable**.

Ok, so what? As Macbeth becomes ever more evil, after committing *regicide*, his lines often become **trochaic**. Like this:

"Told by **an** idiot, **full** of **sound** and **fury, Signify**ing **no**thing"

They usually reveal **psychological** issues the **character** is having, through guilt, lying, becoming evil – etc. Focus on these changes, and you will easily get top grades.

The other change to the **meter** is to give lines more or less than the standard number of feet, or **syllables**. These changes also indicate a **psychological** issue, where the **character** is losing control, and so loses control of the **pentameter**.

At other times, two **characters** will share the **iambic pentameter**, one person speaking say five iambs, and the other speaking the next five. Where the **iambic pentameter** is shared, the **characters** are in agreement and harmony. When the **iambic pentameter** is disrupted, they are out of agreement and harmony. Look out for these when Macbeth is speaking to Lady Macbeth, Banquo and Macduff.

Summarise this in one brilliant sentence.

_____

_____

_____

Shakespeare's Marriage

Shakespeare married his wife, Anne Hathaway, when he was 18 years old. She was 26. She was also 3 months pregnant with his child.

The Patriarchal Society of Elizabethan and *Jacobean* England

Now, let's consider the **subservient role** of women in the **patriarchal society** of the day. Yes, women were considered the property of their husbands by law, but what did that mean in everyday life? Is it likely that the 17 or 18 year old **Shakespeare** seduced Anne, or is it more likely that she took the initiative?

If Shakespeare Loved Anne

When we think this way, we can clearly see why he would write parts for clever, passionate, **powerful** women, like Lady Macbeth. We might **infer** that he did not see women as weaker or **inferior** beings, but men's equal in many respects. And Anne herself would be an odd choice for a highly intelligent, articulate teenager to marry, unless she too were also quick witted and able to keep up with his agile mind.

Moreover, **Shakespeare** was born during the reign of Queen Elizabeth I, a **symbol** of women's **power** and intelligence. We can **infer**, if we choose, that **Shakespeare**'s female leads are a celebration of their intelligence, rather than a warning to husbands that they need to control their wives. In this reading, Lady Macbeth is not a sexist creation to prove that women are manipulative and evil.

If Shakespeare Didn't Love Anne

On the other hand, if we believe that **Shakespeare**'s marriage was forced on him, we might argue that Lady Macbeth represents the **manipulation** of his wife. How likely is it that a 26 year old would get pregnant by accident? How desperate would she be for a baby and a husband in an age where women's **status** was determined entirely by who they marry? How desperate would she be to have a child when the average life expectancy was 35, **because** so many children died young?

We might choose to see the trajectory of Macbeth's marriage, starting as equals with "my dearest partner in greatness" to Macbeth's unemotional reaction to her suicide, "she should have died hereafter", to mirror his own marriage.

Shakespeare's resentment can be **infer**red from his will, "I gyve unto my wief my second best bed with the furniture", which many critics see as a deliberate insult to his wife.

The Value of Friendship in Shakespeare's Life

Shakespeare's first child was called Susanna, and his next children were twins, named Judith and Hamnet. Both appear to have been named after close friends. Hamnet Sadler, a baker, and his wife Judith who were both witness to his will. **Shakespeare** drew the will up aged 52, four weeks before he died. We can **infer** from this that **Shakespeare** believed strongly in loyalty and friendship.

Viewed this way, Macbeth's killing of Banquo is unforgiveable, and much more likely to damage Macbeth than the much more socially damaging *regicide* of Duncan. This helps explain why Macbeth doesn't see Duncan's ghost, he sees only Banquo's ghost.

The Death of Shakespeare's Son, Hamnet

Hamnet died at the age of 11, in 1596. Many scholars wonder what effect this had on **Shakespeare**'s writing.

The **tragedy** of the play could still happen without any **reference** to their child's death. We all believe the **tragedy** begins with his first meeting with the witches. But if **Shakespeare** wanted us to assume it was simply the influence of their evil, **supernatural power**, he would have excluded his child's death.

Introducing this death gives Macbeth and Lady Macbeth **psychological** reasons for their desperate desires. Similarly, if **Shakespeare** simply wanted to portray Lady Macbeth as evil, he would exclude the detail of her child's death. We can clearly see how their grief is partly responsible for both their **tragedies**. So then we can also speculate that this may reflect **Shakespeare**'s own grief at the death of son, Hamnet.

Draw an image in 30 seconds which will help you remember the main ideas.

Label it with 6 key words.

Was Shakespeare a Catholic?

There is a good deal of speculation that **Shakespeare** might have been Catholic. It was illegal to worship as a Catholic in his lifetime, but Richard Davies, the Archdeacon of Lichfield, who knew **Shakespeare**, wrote that **Shakespeare** was a Catholic. We might use this to look at the **plot** of Macbeth. **Shakespeare** creates a 'tyrant king' which acts as a warning of the dangers of tyranny and repression.

This explains Act IV *Scene* 3, which is usually heavily cut in performance (and possibly by your teacher when you read the play!) Why was it so important to **Shakespeare** to have Malcolm pretend to be worse than Macbeth? The whole *scene* is totally unnecessary to the **plot** – we simply need to see Macduff's reaction to his family's death, which sets up his grief and need for revenge.

Here's some of what Malcolm pretends he will do as king:

> "were I king,
> I should cut off the nobles for their lands,
> Desire his jewels and this other's house:
> And my more-having would be as a sauce
> To make me hunger more; that I should forge
> Quarrels unjust against the good and loyal,
> Destroying them for wealth."

Macbeth was written to be performed at the court of King James. He is the main **audience**, and then the nobles at court, not theatre goers. **Therefore**, we might see it as a lesson, played out in front of King James, in an effort to persuade him not to persecute Catholic families following The Gunpowder Plot. This *scene* is asking him not to take their lands and titles, and not use the **plot** as an excuse to become a violent, Machiavellian king.

Next, we might ask how much self-interest there is in this advice, if many of **Shakespeare**'s friends and some of his family are also Catholic.

*Learn this brilliant word. It means using clever, cunning but often dishonest methods that deceive people so that you can win **power** or control.

Summarise this in one brilliant sentence.

_____

_____

_____

_____

Was Shakespeare Homosexual or Bisexual?

Many critics believe that the gender swapping **role**s of so many of his plays, such as *Twelfth Night*, and his **portrayal** of **powerful** women, such as Lady Macbeth, and her demand, "unsex me here", can be explained with **Shakespeare** being homosexual.

Likewise, many of his *sonnets* were love poems written about, and apparently to, men. It is impossible to know, but fun to speculate.

He himself had only three children, two of whom were twins. **Contrast** this to **Shakespeare**'s mother, who had six children, with no twins. This suggests a lack of a sexual relationship with Anne after their first years of marriage.

There were no more children once **Shakespeare** moved to London to write plays and perform in them, and even though he must have returned frequently to Stratford, having more children appears not to have been a priority for him.

Scholars have long puzzled over the **significance** of his will, in which he gave his considerable property to his daughter, Susanna, mentioning Anne in the will only once: "I gyve unto my wief my second best bed with the furniture". We might argue that this distance could be explained by his homosexuality, and this would also explain why he had children so young, while still deciding on his sexual identity.

We might use this to look at the ultra-**masculine** behaviour of Macbeth as a warrior and see **masculinity** itself as his **hamartia**. Lady Macbeth perceives **masculinity** to mean "cruelty" and a lack of "remorse". Both of these allow men to be incredibly single minded and purposeful.

> "unsex me here,
>
> And fill me from the crown to the toe top-full
>
> Of direst cruelty! ...
>
> Come to my woman's breasts,
>
> And take my milk for gall".

Giving this **view** of **masculinity** to Lady Macbeth could be a way for **Shakespeare** to highlight what is wrong with his **society**'s **view** of how men should behave.

King James was Homosexual

If **Shakespeare** were homosexual, it might also explain the popularity of his plays with King James. James became the patron of his acting company, so **Shakespeare** renamed them The King's Players, and they performed frequently at court.

King James financed the first English translation of The Bible, The King James Bible. In 1611, the year of **Shakespeare**'s 46th birthday, Psalm 46 has "shake" as the 46th word, and "spear" as the 46th word from the end. Many critics believe this is a coded birthday message to **Shakespeare**.

Macbeth as a coded message to King James

This would certainly help us assume that Macbeth might also contain coded messages to King James. **Shakespeare** might well have written the play to show the Court the dangers of a king who was too **masculine**. Part of his **motive** might be to persuade the Court to accept James, as an openly homosexual king.

Although homosexuality was frowned on in **society**, King James was quite open about his homosexual affairs. In 1617 he told The House of Lords why he was honouring his lover with the title Earl of Buckingham: "I, James, am neither a god nor an angel, but a man like any other. **Therefore** I act like a man and confess to loving those dear to me more than other men. You may be sure that I love the Earl of Buckingham more than anyone else, and more than you who are here assembled. I wish to speak in my own behalf and not to have it thought to be a defect, for Jesus Christ did the same, and **therefore** I cannot be blamed. Christ had John, and I have George."

Perhaps part of **Shakespeare**'s **motive** was to make **society** at Court more accepting of their new king's sexuality. Perhaps James's patronage of **Shakespeare** was partly based on their shared sexuality.

Summarise this in one brilliant sentence _____
_____
_____
_____

So, **Shakespeare** did not write his plays as an artist, but as a businessman. When we think of literature we imagine a writer drafting and redrafting until the final masterpiece is published. **Shakespeare** didn't have time for that – the public wanted new plays quickly. You might think, **Shakespeare** is our most famous writer. Surely he was the most dedicated to his art?

Yes, and no. He didn't write down the text of his plays to hand on in his will to his family – the plays were instead recreated from memory by actors in his company after **Shakespeare**'s death. Yes, he did publish 18 in his lifetime, but they were not big earners. He made much more money from his **poetry**, which were bound in book form. His plays were simply printed on folded paper, called Folios, ***because*** *they were not made to last.*

We can use this information to argue that **Shakespeare** was incredibly interested in the **context** of his time. His main impulse was probably to give the **audience** what they wanted. Whatever the concerns of the people at the time, and their worries about the politics, war and nobles of the time, would be quickly reflected in his plays.

Did Shakespeare Write to Make Money?

Several times a term, students will tell me that every writer's purpose was to make money. Usually this is not true. Writers tend to write about a passion, often working at other jobs to make money.

But if we go back before the twentieth century, many writers did see themselves as 'smiths' and 'wrights', old Anglo Saxon words which mean maker and worker, rather than artists. They were wordsmiths and playwrights.

In **Shakespeare**'s London, there were 20 theatres with a population of less than 200,000. This is the size of my home town, Swindon, which has only one theatre! So theatre was 20 times more popular than it is now.

Now, a play at the Royal **Shakespeare** Company in Stratford will last around 4 months. In **Shakespeare**'s time the play would be performed just once within two weeks. Then it would be on a rotation with loads of other plays, so it might play once every two weeks for a couple of months, or maybe a year.

No one knows for sure, but what is very clear is that plays were not an art form, they were an entertainment and **Shakespeare** made his money by getting bums on seats. To do that, he had to churn out new plays. So in **Shakespeare**'s case, his purpose really was to make money.

This is still a pretty dumb answer in an essay though. The trick is to explain how what he wrote or portrayed in the play would have appealed to the thoughts, imaginations, feelings, ideas, fashions, concerns and politics at the time. This would then make sure customers paid to come through the doors.

Big Themes in Macbeth

Christian Morality and the Nature of God

God created Adam and Eve in Eden. He forbade them "to eat of the fruit of the Tree of Knowledge of Good and Evil." Satan, in the form of a serpent, tempted Eve to eat the fruit. She was filled with knowledge, and persuaded Adam to eat also.

Because of this, women are traditionally presented as temptresses, luring their men to do things they know they shouldn't do. (This is why Lady Macbeth persuades Macbeth to kill

Duncan). God punished Adam and Eve by banishing them from Eden. (This is why Macbeth and Lady Macbeth never enjoy being king and queen - **Shakespeare** makes sure that they are banished from "joy" and happiness).

Original sin

We are all marked by this crime of Adam and Eve against God. It is called *Original sin*. This means we are all born evil, and must continually strive to be good. (That's why Banquo tries not to get involved in Macbeth's plan, why The weird sisters don't actually tell Macbeth to kill anyone).

Fate and Free Will

God created Eden as an experiment in free will. Could Adam and Eve refuse to be tempted? Could they choose to be good, using their own free will? The answer is no.

They freely chose to go against his command. **However**, he continually allows all men and women to exercise free will for the rest of their lives. Only by choosing to live good lives, and make **moral** choices, can they get back to the state of perfection they had in Eden, and get into Heaven.

We can clearly see this idea of temptation and free will being played out in the choices the Macbeths make about murder.

However, theatre and **tragedy** come to us from the **Greeks**, whose civilisation predated **Christianity**. **Greek** Gods didn't create a **moral** universe in which you would get to heaven by being good. Instead, everyone died and went to the underworld, Hades.

Instead, **Greek** Gods demanded that you worship them with sacrifices, in order to stop the Gods punishing you in some way with bad harvest, shipwreck, disease, etc. **However**, the Gods decided on your **fate** – how and when you would die, and many of the events in your life. In **Greek tragedy** a **character** will find out their **fate** from a *prophecy*. They try to avoid their **fate**, but then whatever they do brings about that **fate** without them knowing it. They can't escape it. Similarly, as a **tragic hero**, Macbeth can't escape his **fate**.

The *Great Chain of Being*

The *Great Chain of Being* was a way of keeping **power** with the rich, and stopping those lower down the **social** ladder asking for more.

The idea was God sat at the top of this chain, then came angels, then the Pope, then kings and queens, then the nobility in all their ranks, then the middle classes (people with wealth but no title), tradesmen, and workers. Then women, then animals, with eagles and lions at the top, down to through less impressive creatures to insects at the bottom.

In medieval times this meant that God decided on everyone's 'station' or **status** in life, and where you sat in the **social** hierarchy. It meant that kings and queens were appointed by God, by "Divine Right", so rebelling against a monarch was a sin against God.

But this also meant that if you were born into a poor family, well, that was pretty much the way it was supposed to be, and you had to respect the lords and ladies who ruled over you.

Constant plagues and exploration of the new world in Elizabethan times meant this belief was being challenged. Suddenly London expanded quite rapidly; it was filled with new businesses, where men could now change their **status**. **Shakespeare** was one typical example, starting as an actor, becoming the country's most successful playwright, but also a really successful businessman and property owner.

The idea of people becoming who they want to be, rather than who they are destined to be by birth, is revolutionary, and it probably started in Elizabethan times.

It is no coincidence that **Shakespeare** invented the **soliloquy** at this time (**although** the **Greeks** got there 2000 years before). Before that, in Britain, the idea that **characters** had rich inner lives, and were **powerful** individuals never found its way on stage. But now that many more people could succeed as individuals, it made sense to show this on stage.

The translation of the **King James Bible** was also revolutionary in this. Suddenly people were able to read the **Bible** and understand its teaching themselves. They didn't have to learn Latin to do it, or depend on priests to explain it to them.

The other attack on the *Great Chain of Being* is that it was mainly a Catholic idea. Once Henry the Eighth converted to Protestantism, and destroyed the monasteries, this 'natural' order looked less certain. The Pope disappeared from it straight away!

This of course led to persecution of Catholics, and to the gunpowder **plot** of 1605, which wouldn't just kill King James, but all the nobility in Parliament as well. This is (almost) the first time that a **plot** against a king had not been led by other nobles, who thought that God had chosen them to be king.

> **Elaborate. How does this remind you of your own life, or the world today?**
>
> _____
>
> _____
>
> _____
>
> _____
>
> _____
>
> _____

The Role of Women in the Patriarchy

(**Patriarchy** – a **society** controlled by men, in their own interests, so that women have limited rights and are **subservient** to males in the form of fathers, husbands, even brothers).

In *Jacobean* society, women were **subservient** to men. They were not even allowed to act on stage, their parts being played by young men. In marriage, a woman was literally her husband's possession, and all that she owned became his. This remained true until the 1870s! With the rich, a father paid a dowry to a suitably rich husband. Marriage for love was a romantic ideal largely ignored by wealthy families, who arranged marriages with other wealthy families. It was **therefore** very common for rich men to have a mistress, women they had actually chosen for themselves.

Women achieved their **status** through marriage, and the **status** of their husband. Within the marriage, their **status** was maintained in the skill of managing the servants and staff of the house, and often the budget. Women were not allowed to own property, unless their husband died. But, as a widow, they were expected to remarry. Single women tended to live with their parents, no matter how old they were. When their parents died, they would not inherit unless she had no brothers.

Added to that, a woman was expected to remain a virgin until marriage. Once married, they might expect to give birth every two years, with an average of 8 children. 30% of these would die by the age of 15.

As you can see, in *Jacobean* England, women had few rights, and their main **role** was as mothers.

When we study Shakespeare we can see the tension between what society expects from the female characters, and what they want for themselves.

It is quite easy to see **Shakespeare** asking for women to have greater **power** and **status** in his plays, attacking **society**'s beliefs.

It is also easy to argue the opposite! When we see Lady Macbeth's **tragic fate**, we can argue this is caused by **Shakespeare**'s beliefs, agreeing with the **society** he lives in, punishing women for breaking the **patriarchal** rules.

How Might These Themes Work in the Thesis to an Essay?

Shakespeare presents Macbeth as a **tragic hero** in order to explore the self-destructive nature of a **patriarchal society**, to serve as a warning to the nobility against the crime of *regicide*, and flatter King James in to maintaining the **social** order without persecuting Catholics.

Having more than one of these in your thesis will force you to argue more than one **viewpoint** in your essay, and force the examiner to consider whether it is worth a **Grade 7** .

Go back over this whole section and pick out the top 5 ideas you need to remember.
1._____ _____
2._____ _____ _____
3._____ _____
4._____ _____
5._____

A desert place. [*Thunder and lightning. Enter three Witches*]

First Witch. When shall we three meet again
In thunder, lightning, or in rain?

Second Witch. When the hurlyburly's done,
When the battle's lost and won.**5**

Third Witch. That will be ere the set of sun.

First Witch. Where the place?

Second Witch. Upon the heath.

Third Witch. There to meet with Macbeth.

First Witch. I come, Graymalkin!**10**

Second Witch. Paddock calls.

Third Witch. Anon.

All. Fair is foul, and foul is fair:
Hover through the fog and filthy air.

[Exeunt]

Key Question

Why does Shakespeare begin the play with the weird sisters?

Grade 6 **Shakespeare** deliberately places the witches at the beginning in order to tap into King James's fascination with witchcraft, which all *Jacobeans* would have known about following James's publication of his book on witchcraft, *Daemonologie*.

They appear to be in control of the weather, asking when they will next meet, "In thunder, lightning, or in rain?" This plays to King James's belief that witches conjured a storm to try to sink a ship he was travelling on, and could control the weather.

Grade 7

Apart from introducing this main **theme** of **supernatural** evil, **Shakespeare** also uses them to introduce the idea of **paradox** and deception. **Therefore** the witches describe reality as "Fair is foul, and foul is fair", so that nothing is what it seems.

This prepares the ground for Macbeth looking like "the innocent flower" but being "the serpent under't". It **foreshadows** the thane of Cawdor disguising that he is a "traitor", so Duncan never suspects him. It helps us realise that the witches' *prophecy* that Macbeth will be "king hereafter" can be both "fair" and "foul", **because** it leads to *regicide*. Shakespeare **therefore** creates a world which is untrustworthy and uncertain.

Grade 8

Macbeth, of course, is a play reacting to political events of the day. James is a foreign king, who has just survived a daring and far reaching assassination attempt from what we would now call religious extremists, a group of Catholic plotters. The idea that further cells of plotters might exist all across London is only natural. Anyone could be a secret plotter, a traitor. Added to that, Queen Elizabeth had no heir. Many nobles would **view** their claim to the throne as no worse than James', so that he was another "step [they] must o'erleap", which meant they would need to assassinate him.

So **Shakespeare** reflects all that uncertainty, and also tries to show a clear way forward, through noble kingship restoring order after the cautionary tale of the **tragic hero**, Macbeth. **However**, in doing so, **Shakespeare** might look at the fear of witchcraft as another symptom of a **society** which is lurching towards paranoia rather than peace and prosperity.

Firstly, notice how he gives the witches a different **meter** to their lines:

"**When** the **hur**ly**bur**ly's **done**,
When the **bat**tle's **lost** and **won**."

They are seven **syllables** long, and the first **syllable** is **stress** ed, so it is **trochaic**, rather than **iambic**. They are **trochaic tetrameter**. This marks the witches as different from the other **characters**. We can argue that the **trochee** is a sign of their evil. **Shakespeare** will use it to show a **character**'s evil thoughts later in the play, when they switch to it from an **iambic meter**.

Grade 9

Tracy Borman, writing for the BBC's magazine, History Extra, quotes King James's *Daemonologie*:

"James's beliefs had a dangerously misogynistic core. He grew up to scorn – even revile – women... He took every opportunity to propound the **view** that they were far more likely than men to succumb to witchcraft. "**As that sex is frailer than man is, so is it easier to be entrapped in these gross snares of the Devil**," he argued in *Daemonologie*, "*as was overwell proved to be true by the Serpent's deceiving of Eve at the beginning which makes him the friendlier with that sex since then.*" He would later commission a new version of the Bible in which all **references** to witches were rewritten in the female gender."

We can easily see how **Shakespeare** uses this **description** of women in his creation of Lady Macbeth, who uses the same **imagery** of the "Serpent" when persuading Macbeth to murder. She will be shown to be "frailer" when she commits suicide through guilt and madness. She will fear "hell" more than Macbeth **because**, as James would say, she is trapped by the "snares of the Devil".

In **contrast**, Queen Elizabeth had not punished witchcraft. Witches were only punished if they had committed a crime, for example using witchcraft to murder someone. Under James, a witch did not actually need to have harmed anyone – they could be executed simply for being suspected of being a witch. For this reason, witchcraft was used as a reason to execute witches at twice the rate in Scotland compared to England.

> **Write 3 sentences. Use the words highlighted in the notes (as these are subject terminology).**
>
> _____
>
> _____
>
> _____
>
> _____
>
> _____
>
> _____
>
> _____
>
> _____
>
> _____

Beyond Grade 9

This is important **because** it gives us evidence to suppose that **Shakespeare** himself would have good reason not to believe in the **power** of witches and witchcraft. It gives us an insight in to why he would feel the need to flatter King James by including witches, but also why he might write a play in which the witches are a red herring, a false clue. The real culprits here are Macbeth and Lady Macbeth, who choose to take actions on their own.

But the **trochaic tetrameter** the witches speak in also has a very childish **rhythm**. **Shakespeare** adds to this with the constant **repetition** of "when", the **alliteration** of "b" and "l". The simple **rhyming couplet**s, the childlike, almost made up word "hurlyburly", all combine to suggest that the witches may not be as **powerful** as they seem and are in fact a simple, childlike fear.

This **motif** of childlike fear is constantly picked up on in the play. Lady Macbeth will complain to Macbeth that he is like a child, fearing a "painted devil". Here, the sense of a childlike world is invoked when **Shakespeare** ends the _scene_ with "Hover through the fog and filthy air." This refers to the witches' ability to fly. Spend a minute thinking about this – none of the **characters** mention seeing the witches fly. In **Shakespeare**'s lifetime, you might be very sceptical of anyone claiming to have seen women fly on their broomsticks. It is a childlike idea, suited to story, rather than fact.

Another way **Shakespeare** makes belief in witches seem childlike is in the witches' conversation with their _familiars_ (animals believed to be the form taken by a demon).

>   **First Witch.** I come, Graymalkin!
>
>   **Second Witch.** Paddock calls.

These suggest that the witches are controlled by their demon *familiars*. But the **audience** never hear them. Even more significantly, neither do the other witches – the second witch has to explain that "Paddock" is calling her, **because** the first witch clearly cannot hear "Paddock".

Again, this raises the possibility that there are no such things, that these are simply figments of the witches' imaginations. **Shakespeare** will play with this idea repeatedly, when Macbeth sees the "dagger of the mind" and the "horrible shadow" (Banquo's ghost), and Lady Macbeth will imagine the "damned spot" of blood she cannot remove from her hand.

Finally, it is worth noting that **Shakespeare** never names the witches as witches during the play, but only ever refers to them as "the weird sisters", which were the names for the *Norns* or Fates in **Norse mythology**. Here **Shakespeare** again suggests that witchcraft is not a real **power**, though **fate** might be. Macbeth's **tragedy** is how he interferes with his **fate**, rather than the weird sisters making him do anything.

Draw an image in 30 seconds which will help you remember the main ideas.

Label it with 6 key words.

Write 3 sentences. The first words of each one must be in this order. BECAUSE, BUT, SO.

_____

_____

_____

_____

_____

_____

_____

_____

_____

Act I, *Scene* 2

A camp near Forres

[Alarum within. Enter DUNCAN, MALCOLM, DONALBAIN,] [p]LENNOX, with Attendants, meeting a bleeding Sergeant]

Duncan. What bloody man is that? He can report,
As seemeth by his plight, of the revolt
The newest state.**20**

Malcolm. This is the sergeant
Who like a good and hardy soldier fought
'Gainst my captivity. Hail, brave friend!
Say to the king the knowledge of the broil
As thou didst leave it.**25**

Sergeant. Doubtful it stood;
As two spent swimmers, that do cling together
And choke their art. The merciless Macdonwald—
Worthy to be a rebel, for to that
The multiplying villanies of nature **30**
Do swarm upon him—from the western isles
Of kerns and gallowglasses is supplied;
And fortune, on his damned quarrel smiling,
Show'd like a rebel's whore: but all's too weak:
For brave Macbeth—well he deserves that name— **35**
Disdaining fortune, with his brandish'd steel,
Which smoked with bloody execution,
Like valour's minion carved out his passage
Till he faced the slave;
Which ne'er shook hands, nor bade farewell to him, **40**
Till he unseam'd him from the nave to the chaps,
And fix'd his head upon our battlements.

Duncan. O valiant cousin! worthy gentleman!

Sergeant. As whence the sun 'gins his reflection
Shipwrecking storms and direful thunders break, **45**
So from that spring whence comfort seem'd to come
Discomfort swells. Mark, king of Scotland, mark:
No sooner justice had with valour arm'd
Compell'd these skipping kerns to trust their heels,
But the Norweyan lord surveying vantage, **50**
With furbish'd arms and new supplies of men
Began a fresh assault.

Duncan. Dismay'd not this
Our captains, Macbeth and Banquo?

Sergeant. Yes; **55**
As sparrows eagles, or the hare the lion.
If I say sooth, I must report they were
As cannons overcharged with double cracks, so they
Doubly redoubled strokes upon the foe:
Except they meant to bathe in reeking wounds, **60**
Or memorise another Golgotha,
I cannot tell.
But I am faint, my gashes cry for help.

Duncan. So well thy words become thee as thy wounds;
They smack of honour both. Go get him surgeons. **65**
[Exit Sergeant, attended]

Key Question

Is Macbeth the victim of a martial society [*one devoted to war*] or is he a psychopath?

Grade 6

Shakespeare introduces Macbeth as a **heroic** warrior. He is brave, "disdaining fortune" in battle. He is skilful and ruthless, so his sword "smoked with bloody execution." He is fierce and strong, able to "unseam" an enemy "from the nave to the chaps". Most importantly, this victim is Macdonwald, a leader of the Scottish rebels.

Like the sergeant, *Jacobeans* would have been impressed by Macbeth's strength and ferocity in battle, executing Macdonwald, so that "he unseam'd him from the nave to the chaps". At the beginning **Shakespeare portrays** him as a true **hero**, so that his fall will be more **tragic**. This will also imply that his **hamartia** is incredibly **powerful**, which will help **Shakespeare** to suggest that the witches control a **powerful** evil.

Grade 7

The Sergeant describes a well-known phenomenon with survivors in a war. Survival amid chaos and carnage leads to feelings of invincibility. He describes Macbeth as "Disdaining fortune, with his brandish'd steel, / Which smoked with bloody execution". In this **view** of "fortune" we can see a man who believes he can create his own **fate**, no matter how the odds are stacked against him. He is an efficient killer, so that his sword "smoked with bloody execution". This **metaphor** conveys both the speed of his swordplay, and suggests his many victims, **because** the blood is still warm enough to smoke. "Execution" further suggests he is able to move to his next enemy speedily.

This foreshadows Macbeth's belief that he can bring about his own **fate** once he hears the witches' prophecies, and it also provides a reason for his belief that "none of woman born" can harm him. Given his experience in battle, this might even seem logical.

Next we see him revelling in this sense of invincibility, and taking his time over the "execution" of Macdonwald. Here he acts like a man who revels in violence, the victim's pain and blood. The sergeant is not horrified by this **psychopathic** behaviour, but full of admiration as Macbeth fought:

"Till he faced the slave;
Which ne'er shook hands, nor bade farewell to him,
Till he unseam'd him from the nave to the chaps".

This killing cannot happen at arm's length. To "unseam" his enemy Macbeth must pierce him at the "nave", his navel, and then slice upwards, through stomach, sternum, chest and then to the chin, in one motion. This would be almost impossible with a sword, but demand closer quarters. A knife could do this, provided Macbeth held his victim to prevent him pulling away or falling forward. Then we discover that he must keep Macdonwald upright and facing him while he butchers him, **because** at the end he "shook hands" with the dying man and, "bade him farewell" with pitiless **humour**.

When Macbeth speaks later about wading in a river of "blood", he first enters the **metaphorical** river here, where he is literally covered in the blood of his enemies. His murderous instincts **therefore** don't start with Duncan.

What are the 3 main ideas you want to remember so far?

1._____

_____

2._____

_____

3._____

_____

Grade 8

However, Macbeth is not criticised for this. It is not till the end of the play that Malcolm calls Macbeth a "butcher". This suggests that this **martial society** glorifies war, the violence of the warrior. This emotional detachment towards killing is much prized and we might argue that Macbeth's **tragedy** is that he has been conditioned this way.

Grade 9

The sergeant imagines Macbeth and Banquo fighting as though "they meant to bathe in reeking wounds, / Or memorise another Golgotha". This **metaphor** reveals his personal, perhaps unconscious disgust. The wounds of his enemies are 'reeking' which carried one meaning of giving off smoke. This is **juxtaposed** with the horror of Macbeth and Banquo bathing in blood. They actually "bathe" in the "wounds", implying they are now relishing the killing **because** it is immediate and tactile; they literally have a feel for it.

The **reference** to "Golgotha" is deeply **ambiguous** and **foreshadows** the **theme** of *equivocation* or falseness in the play. According to all four of the gospels, Golgotha is the hill on which Jesus and two other prisoners were crucified. Firstly, the blood spilled at "Golgotha" belonged to Jesus, and **therefore** Macbeth and Banquo are described as **metaphorically** anti-**Christian** in their spilling of blood. While the sergeant wants his **audience** to see Macbeth's defence of Scotland as godly, **Shakespeare** suggests the reverse. Their enjoyment of killing is unholy.

This is also brought out in the Biblical account, where a Roman soldier taunts Jesus, making him wear a crown of thorns, and piercing his side with a spear. The **allusion** to the biblical Roman soldier clearly **portrays** the soldiers Macbeth and Banquo as unholy and evil in their spilling of blood.

Write 3 sentences. The first words of each one must be in this order. BECAUSE, BUT, SO.

_____

_____

_____

_____

_____

_____

Beyond Grade 9

The sergeant supposes that they are trying to "memorise" this. His first meaning is 'commemorate' here. Like Jesus, Macbeth and Banquo are willing to give up their lives as Jesus did, to save Scotland as Jesus saved mankind. **However**, "memorise" strongly suggests that they are creating **powerful** memories. They "bathe in reeking wounds" so that they will be able to "bathe" in joyful memories of the slaughter.

Because both Banquo and Macbeth are portrayed as **psychopathic** in this way, we might **infer** that **Shakespeare** is criticising the **martial** nature of this **society**, rather than attacking Macbeth specifically. Nevertheless, we can clearly see that this bloodlust is Macbeth's **hamartia**. It is **ironic** that his fatal flaw is the unfortunate gift which gives him such great success as a warrior.

Shakespeare deliberately explores this issue with the final lines of the _scene_s, "So well thy words become thee as thy wounds; / They smack of honour both. Go get him surgeons". Here King Duncan sees the glorification of bloodlust as noble, an "honour" equal to the physical battle which has resulted in his "wounds". He recognises the importance of this kind of propaganda in building fearless warriors who will save Scotland from invasion. **Shakespeare** uses this to point out what is wrong with this **society**, and then adds **irony** to this – the king who glorifies bloodlust will fall victim to it almost immediately.

Shakespeare is also careful to remind us of this at the end with the introduction of Old Siward. He is created so that he can give us his reaction to the death of his son. He is proud that his son died with is wounds on his "front", bravely fighting Macbeth. But the true mark of his glorification of bloodlust is that he refuses to feel any "sorrow" for his son's death, explaining "he is worth no more" and **character**ising him as "God's soldier".

Perhaps **Shakespeare** wants to point out that this callous **view** of warfare is deluded, and will always breed future Macbeths, "butcher"(s) addicted to slaughter.

Summarise this in one brilliant sentence.

_____

_____

_____

Draw an image in 30 seconds which will help you remember the main ideas.

Label it with 6 key words.

Write 3 sentences. Use the words highlighted in the notes (as these are subject terminology).

_____

_____

_____

_____

_____

_____

_____

_____

_____

_____

_____

A heath near Forres.

[Thunder. Enter the three Witches]

First Witch. Look what I have.

Second Witch. Show me, show me.**125**

First Witch. Here I have a pilot's thumb,
Wreck'd as homeward he did come.

[Drum within]

Third Witch. A drum, a drum!
Macbeth doth come.**130**

All. The weird sisters, hand in hand,
Posters of the sea and land,
Thus do go about, about:
Thrice to thine and thrice to mine
And thrice again, to make up nine. **135**
Peace! the charm's wound up.

[Enter MACBETH and BANQUO]

Macbeth. So foul and fair a day I have not seen.

Banquo. How far is't call'd to Forres? What are these
So wither'd and so wild in their attire, **140**
That look not like the inhabitants o' the earth,
And yet are on't? Live you? or are you aught
That man may question? You seem to understand me,
By each at once her chappy finger laying
Upon her skinny lips: you should be women, **145**
And yet your beards forbid me to **interpret**
That you are so.

Macbeth. Speak, if you can: what are you?

First Witch. All hail, Macbeth! hail to thee, thane of Glamis!

Second Witch. All hail, Macbeth, hail to thee, thane of Cawdor!**150**

Third Witch. All hail, Macbeth, thou shalt be king hereafter!

Banquo. Good sir, why do you start; and seem to fear
Things that do sound so fair? I' the name of truth,
Are ye fantastical, or that indeed
Which outwardly ye show? My noble partner **155**

You greet with present grace and great prediction
Of noble having and of royal hope,
That he seems rapt withal: to me you speak not.
If you can look into the seeds of time,
And say which grain will grow and which will not, **160**
Speak then to me, who neither beg nor fear
Your favours nor your hate.

First Witch. Hail!

Second Witch. Hail!

Third Witch. Hail!**165**

First Witch. Lesser than Macbeth, and greater.

Second Witch. Not so happy, yet much happier.

Third Witch. Thou shalt get kings, though thou be none:
So all hail, Macbeth and Banquo!

First Witch. Banquo and Macbeth, all hail!**170**

Macbeth. Stay, you imperfect speakers, tell me more:
By Sinel's death I know I am thane of Glamis;
But how of Cawdor? the thane of Cawdor lives,
A prosperous gentleman; and to be king
Stands not within the prospect of belief, **175**
No more than to be Cawdor. Say from whence
You owe this strange intelligence? or why
Upon this blasted heath you stop our way
With such prophetic greeting? Speak, I charge you.

[Witches vanish]

Banquo. The earth hath bubbles, as the water has,
And these are of them. Whither are they vanish'd?

Macbeth. Into the air; and what seem'd corporal melted
As breath into the wind. Would they had stay'd!

Banquo. Were such things here as we do speak about? **185**
Or have we eaten on the insane root
That takes the reason prisoner?

Macbeth. Your children shall be kings.

Banquo. You shall be king.

Macbeth. And thane of Cawdor too: went it not so?**190**

Banquo. To the selfsame tune and words. Who's here?

[Enter ROSS and ANGUS]

Ross. The king hath happily received, Macbeth,
The news of thy success; and when he reads
Thy personal venture in the rebels' fight, **195**
His wonders and his praises do contend
Which should be thine or his: silenced with that,
In **view**ing o'er the rest o' the selfsame day,
He finds thee in the stout Norweyan ranks,
Nothing afeard of what thyself didst make, **200**
Strange **image**s of death. As thick as hail
Came post with post; and every one did bear
Thy praises in his kingdom's great defence,
And pour'd them down before him.

Angus. We are sent **205**
To give thee from our royal master thanks;
Only to herald thee into his sight,
Not pay thee.

Ross. And, for an earnest of a greater honour,
He bade me, from him, call thee thane of Cawdor: **210**
In which addition, hail, most worthy thane!
For it is thine.

Banquo. What, can the devil speak true?

Macbeth. The thane of Cawdor lives: why do you dress me
In borrow'd robes?**215**

Angus. Who was the thane lives yet;
But under heavy judgment bears that life
Which he deserves to lose. Whether he was combined
With those of Norway, or did line the rebel
With hidden help and vantage, or that with both **220**
He labour'd in his country's wreck, I know not;
But treasons capital, confess'd and proved,
Have overthrown him.

Macbeth. *[Aside]* Glamis, and thane of Cawdor!
The greatest is behind. **225**
[To ROSS and ANGUS]
Thanks for your pains.
[To BANQUO]
Do you not hope your children shall be kings,
When those that gave the thane of Cawdor to me **230**
Promised no less to them?

Banquo. That trusted home
Might yet enkindle you unto the crown,
Besides the thane of Cawdor. But 'tis strange:
And oftentimes, to win us to our harm, **235**
The instruments of darkness tell us truths,
Win us with honest trifles, to betray's
In deepest consequence.
Cousins, a word, I pray you.

Macbeth. *[Aside]*. Two truths are told, **240**
As happy prologues to the swelling act
Of the imperial **theme**.—I thank you, gentlemen.
[Aside] This **supernatural** soliciting]
Cannot be ill, cannot be good: if ill,
Why hath it given me earnest of success, **245**
Commencing in a truth? I am thane of Cawdor:
If good, why do I yield to that suggestion
Whose horrid **image** doth unfix my hair
And make my seated heart knock at my ribs,
Against the use of nature? Present fears **250**
Are less than horrible imaginings:
My thought, whose murder yet is but fantastical,
Shakes so my single state of man that function
Is smother'd in surmise, and nothing is
But what is not.**255**

Banquo. Look, how our partner's rapt.

Macbeth. *[Aside]* If chance will have me king, why, chance may crown me,
Without my stir.

Banquo. New horrors come upon him,
Like our strange garments, cleave not to their mould **260**
But with the aid of use.

Macbeth. *[Aside]* Come what come may,
Time and the hour runs through the roughest day.

This is the most crucial scene in the play because it prepares the scene for every future event.

Key Question

How far do the witches influence Macbeth's decision to commit *regicide* by killing Duncan?

Grade 6

Third Witch. All hail, Macbeth, thou shalt be king hereafter!

Banquo. Good sir, why do you start; and seem to fear
Things that do sound so fair?

The witches **manipulate** Macbeth by telling him he will be "king hereafter". We know this works immediately, **because** Banquo notices that he seems "to fear" this *prophecy*, even though it should "sound so fair." **Shakespeare contrasts** this reaction to Banquo, who obviously doesn't start to think of murder. This is necessary, **because Shakespeare** needs to flatter King James, who believed he was descended from the original Banquo.

Grade 7

Shakespeare also suggests that the witches know Macbeth can be influenced to commit evil acts. This is revealed in their use of "thou" rather than the **formal** 'you'. This **direct address** is in**formal**, and shows that the witches believe that they are Macbeth's equal.

The first point **Shakespeare** wants us to realise is that the witches have no **power** over Macbeth, nor indeed any other man. They seek desperately to influence Macbeth and Banquo, but to do so rely on human error, not **supernatural power**. **Consequently**, the first witch shows off her prize ingredient in her charm, "Here I have a pilot's thumb, / Wreck'd as homeward he did come." **Shakespeare** deliberately prevents the witch saying 'I' "wreck'd". Far from claiming a part in this "wreck" the **emphasis** is on "he". The pilot is responsible for safe passage, but has failed to do so through poor decision making. This is what she needs from Macbeth – poor decision making.

The shipwreck is an **allusion** to King James' belief that witches conjured a storm to sink his ship. On the surface, of course, **Shakespeare** includes the witches to flatter King James's interest in **prose**cuting witches. But beneath the surface we'll see that **Shakespeare** attributes no **supernatural power** to the witches other than *prophecy*.

Grade 8

The riddles they will speak in are an **allusion** to the tradition of **Greek myth**s in which **heroes** are the victims of *prophecy*. Tiresias had the gift of *prophecy*, but was at one stage punished by the gods by being turned into a woman. We can clearly trace an **allusion** to this with the "beards" which the witches have. They have been punished in a **patriarchal society** which values female beauty. Their ugliness is a punishment they might not deserve and so perhaps this causes them to turn to witchcraft.

Shakespeare plays with other elements of **Greek tragedy** where *prophecy* is closely linked to **fate**. **Heroes** went out of their way to avoid their **fate**, and the actions which they took unwittingly brought it about. So, Oedipus hears a *prophecy* that he will kill his father. He **therefore** flees his country, not realising that he is adopted. In the new country, he ends up killing his real father. **Shakespeare** inverts this idea, and makes sure that Macbeth runs towards his **fate**, becoming king. His **tragedy** is that his **fate** is not worth having.

Grade 9

Shakespeare also has in mind the three **Fates**, or **Norns** in **Norse myth**, the three **Moirai**, women of **Greek myth**, who decided on the **fates** of every mortal. In this **allusion** there is no possibility that Macbeth can avoid his **fate**. It suggests he will definitely become king, **because** the Fates were never wrong. His **tragedy** is that he does not wait for this to happen naturally.

But again, this undermines the idea of the "weird sisters" as witches. We realise that Macbeth never calls them witches. This again undermines their **supernatural power** as a cause of

Macbeth's behaviour. Instead they simply have the gift of ***prophecy***, seeing the future. This is important to **Shakespeare** for two reasons. Firstly, he is writing a **tragedy**, in the tradition of **Greek tragedy**, where **heroes** like Odysseus cannot escape their **fate**. Secondly, he is creating a new art form, in which **characters** explore both their individuality and their innermost thoughts.

> **Third Witch.** All hail, Macbeth, thou shalt be king hereafter!

> **Banquo.** Good sir, why do you start; and seem to fear
> Things that do sound so fair?

Macbeth has an instinctive fear of this gift of ***prophecy***. One possibility is that as soon as the weird sisters tell him he shall "be king hereafter" he realises that this **fate** will have a price to pay, a price he fears. The other possibility, as we saw in the Grade 6 section, is that he immediately fantasises about killing Duncan, and fears his own bloodlust and **blasphemous** attack on God's appointed king.

> "**Third Witch.** Thou shalt get kings, though thou be none:
> So all hail, Macbeth and Banquo!"

Banquo has no fear of the weird sisters' ***prophecy***, and simply asks them to tell him his own future. They tell Banquo he will "get kings", meaning beget them, meaning he will be the ancestor of kings, beginning with Fleance.

When Macbeth plans to kill Banquo, there is little logic to his plan. Firstly, **because** the witches just reveal **fate**, and **fate** cannot be escaped. Secondly, Macbeth has no children, and **therefore** has no legacy to protect. **Shakespeare** want us to know this, which is why he makes Duncan announce his successor. This happens to be Duncan's son Malcolm, but such a choice is not inevitable.

This is important to the dramatist who wants us to understand the **psychology** of Macbeth in a way which was unthinkable just thirty years before. Then, **morality plays** contained **characters** who faced simplistic choices between good and evil. **Shakespeare** developed **soliloquys** in a world which was used to the **morality play** to show the **psychology** behind action in a new kind of play. He wanted us to invest in his **character**'s thoughts and **motives**.

What are the 3 main ideas you want to remember so far?

1._____

_____

2._____

_____

3._____

_____

Beyond grade 9

> By Sinel's death I know I am thane of Glamis;
> But how of Cawdor? the thane of Cawdor lives,
> A prosperous gentleman;

Shakespeare recreates a universe in which promotion is based on death. Macbeth has become "thane of Glamis" through the death of Sinel. This does not suggest an inheritance of the title, but one that has been given to him after military victory. Now he has become "thane of Cawdor" he is puzzled. The pattern is clear in his mind – he acquires titles only when the previous thane has died. So he might logically think that the most likely way for him to get the new title of king would be to kill the existing king.

This is a natural consequence of ruling in a **martial society**. This play urges King James' court not to return to a **martial society**, but to remain a political one. He isn't just relying on the **Christian interpretation** of The *Great Chain of Being*, or the doctrine of *Divine Right of Kings* to stop the nobles thinking of killing King James. Instead he is pointing out the terrible instability of titles won by force.

Becoming thane of Cawdor also proves the witches have a gift of *prophecy*. Their **supernatural power** is to see into the future. But do they also have a **supernatural power** to make Macbeth act in evil ways? The conventional **interpretation** is that his **contemporary audience**, and King James, would think they do. **However**, Shakespeare rejects that, and looks at the **psychology** of the man.

Grade 6

Banquo asks, "What, can the devil speak true?" This is often **interpreted** as Banquo refusing to act on the weird sisters' prophecies, **because** he believes they are witches, with **satanic power**.

Grade 7

However, a more logical **interpretation** is that he believes the devil cannot "speak true". **Therefore** the prophecies are not evil, they are just statements of future facts. This is important, **because** it means he can trust them when they tell him Fleance will be king. This is delightfully *ironic*. Banquo was believed to be King James's ancestor, and is **therefore** presented in a noble light. The real Banquo helped the real Macbeth to kill the real Duncan. Here, **Shakespeare** makes him an even more noble **character**, **because** he needs to teach the court that *regicide* is wrong. No doubt King James would appreciate this change of **historical** fact.

Grade 8

But the consequence of this is that **Shakespeare** presents Fleance's kingship (and **therefore** King James's accession to the throne of Scotland) as brought about by the witches. They begin the chain of events which lead to Macbeth murdering Duncan, Macduff killing Macbeth and, presumably, Fleance overcoming Malcolm. Such an **interpretation** is not flattering to King James, which is another reason **Shakespeare** is so keen to question the **power** of witchcraft and **emphasise** Macbeth's **psychological flaws** rather than the weird sisters' influence.

What are the 2 main ideas you want to remember so far?
1._____   _____   2._____   _____

Shakespeare gives us a sense of Macbeth's insecurity. He rejects the title of thane of Cawdor, "The thane of Cawdor lives: why do you dress me / In borrow'd robes?" This is the **metaphor** of a man who has not been born into **power**, but has had to seize it by military force. Macbeth is a man who knows he has been playing a part, writing his own script in order to improve his **status** and fortune. This is a strong parallel with **Shakespeare**, who has done the same, literally writing his own scripts to change his own fortune.

By the end of the play, Macbeth takes this **metaphor** a step further. He sees that men are "merely players" and the script they are following is "a tale, told by an idiot." When we get there we will consider how much of this is an attack against himself for writing his own script, and how much an attack on God for His creation of **fate**. At this stage we can clearly see that Macbeth is never wholly comfortable with promotion. His new **status** always feels like "borrow'd robes". He feels insecure. This will explain his need to kill Banquo, who will demand the "robes" for his son.

Banquo's warning to Macbeth is fascinating:

> "But 'tis strange:
> And oftentimes, to win us to our harm, **235**
> The instruments of darkness tell us truths,
> Win us with honest trifles, to betray's (11 **syllables**)
> In deepest consequence. (7 **syllables**)
>
> Cousins, a word, I pray you." (6 **syllables**)

Grade 6

The obvious **interpretation** is that Banquo knows Macbeth very well, and suspects he will begin to **plot** how to become king. This is the "deepest consequence" which he wants Macbeth to avoid.

Grade 7

However, we can also see two **psychological** tricks Banquo plays on Macbeth here. The first is to call the new title of thane of Cawdor an "honest trifle". This clearly suggests that it is not really worth having in comparison to being king. So Banquo doesn't really suggest that Macbeth should wait to become king naturally, in time. He suggests that settling for being "Cawdor" is to accept something nearly worthless.

Banquo's next trick is to leave this thought hanging, to work on Macbeth's **psyche**. If he wanted to dissuade Macbeth, he would discuss it further with him, and labour the point that to be king is his destiny – he need only wait for it to happen, just as becoming thane of Cawdor just happened. But instead, he abruptly leaves the conversation to speak to the messengers.

Grade 8

Shakespeare often reveals a **character**'s disturbed **psychological** state by breaking **iambic pentameter**, which is exactly what happens here. Even with the **elision** of "betray's", the line has 11 **syllables**, and the next line only 7. This implies a dishonesty in Banquo's words, which on the surface warn against *regicide*. But the broken **pentameter** suggests he is deceiving Macbeth, actually encouraging Macbeth to consider the benefits of not settling for "trifles".

Shakespeare does the same when Macbeth first speaks of killing Duncan. It is such a horrible thought that he cannot bring himself to name it:

> "If good, why do I yield to that suggestion (11 **syllables**)
> Whose horrid image doth unfix my hair
> And make my seated heart knock at my ribs,
> Against the use of nature?"

Notice that the first line is made 11 **syllables** long. **Shakespeare** could have used "**image**" instead of "suggestion" to make it 10 **syllables**. This lack of control **emphasises** that Macbeth is thinking of *regicide*, and that Banquo's tactics have worked. It isn't just the witches who are making this "suggestion".

What are the 3 main ideas you want to remember so far?

1._____

_____

2._____

_____

3._____

_____

Beyond Grade 9

We also get a sense that Macbeth is happiest when running toward danger as he did in battle. Traditionally, we might expect the idea of his hair standing on end, and his heart knocking at his "ribs" to be reasons to avoid *regicide*. His body is already rebelling "against the use of nature" in killing the king.

Instead he describes his hair being unfixed, as though liberated. Even in **Shakespeare**'s time most people followed in the same **role**s as their parents. It further suggests his **perspective** as a self-made man which, in Macbeth's **feudal society**, would usually only be possible through military success. Macbeth's **social status** has not been fixed. He has been able to rise through the ranks of thanes **because** of his military skill.

Another clue is that part of the attraction of being a soldier is his delight in action. Without this fear, he has a "seated heart", which is both contented but bored. The **personification** of it knocking against his ribs is also fascinating. First it is full of action. Secondly, it is a rising movement, which we can again link to his desire for higher **status**. Thirdly, the knock is also a demand for admittance – Macbeth wants to get out of his current state in order to enter the new one of kingship.

Fear **therefore** provides him both with excitement and opportunity, so he rushes towards it. We will be reminded of this when Malcolm's army attack him, and he observes nostalgically, "I have almost forgot the taste of fears." **However**, he resolves not to act at this stage. Attractive though this fear is, he knows *regicide* is a risk he does not have to take – he can simply wait to become king.

> "If chance will have me king, why, chance may crown me, (11 **syllables**)
> Without my stir. (4 **syllables**)
>
> **Banquo.** New horrors come upon him". (7 **syllables**)

Banquo watches Macbeth thinking. It is interesting that when Macbeth might be expected to show relief and resolution in this decision to allow **fate** and "chance" to "crown" him, Banquo sees the opposite. His friend's expression looks like "New horrors". Waiting is horrifying to Macbeth.

This raises an interesting possibility about Macbeth's **hamartia**. Most will probably argue it is his ambition. But Macbeth and Banquo's words suggest another possibility. What attracts him is not **status**, but the violent action necessary to win it. **Shakespeare** also offers us a further clue again through the disruption of **pentameter**, where "upon" adds an extra **syllable** to the line Banquo and Macbeth share, where 'to' would have easily given 10 **syllables**, and "why" takes the line to 11 **syllables**.

Build Long Term Memory!

Summarise this in one brilliant sentence.

_____

_____

_____

_____

_____

Write 3 sentences. Use the words highlighted in the notes (as these are subject terminology).

_____

_____

_____

_____

_____

_____

_____

_____

_____

_____

_____

Write 3 sentences. The first words of each one must be in this order. BECAUSE, BUT, SO.

_____

_____

_____

_____

_____

_____

_____

_____

_____

_____

Draw an image in 30 seconds which will help you remember the main ideas.

Label it with 6 key words.

Inverness. Macbeth's castle.

[Enter LADY MACBETH, reading a letter]

Lady Macbeth. 'They met me in the day of success: and I have **345**
learned by the perfectest report, they have more in
them than mortal knowledge. When I burned in desire
to question them further, they made themselves air,
into which they vanished. Whiles I stood rapt in
the wonder of it, came missives from the king, who **350**
all-hailed me 'thane of Cawdor;' by which title,
before, these weird sisters saluted me, and referred
me to the coming on of time, with 'Hail, king that
shalt be!' This have I thought good to deliver
thee, my dearest partner of greatness, that thou **355**
mightst not lose the dues of rejoicing, by being
ignorant of what greatness is promised thee. Lay it
to thy heart, and farewell.'
Glamis thou art, and Cawdor; and shalt be
What thou art promised: yet do I fear thy nature; **360**
It is too full o' the milk of human kindness
To catch the nearest way: thou wouldst be great;
Art not without ambition, but without
The illness should attend it: what thou wouldst highly,
That wouldst thou holily; wouldst not play false, **365**
And yet wouldst wrongly win: thou'ldst have, great Glamis,
That which cries 'Thus thou must do, if thou have it;
And that which rather thou dost fear to do
Than wishest should be undone.' Hie thee hither,
That I may pour my spirits in thine ear; **370**
And chastise with the valour of my tongue
All that impedes thee from the golden round,
Which **fate** and metaphysical aid doth seem
To have thee crown'd withal.

[Enter a Messenger] **375**
What is your tidings?

Messenger. The king comes here to-night.

Lady Macbeth. Thou'rt mad to say it:
Is not thy master with him? who, were't so,
Would have inform'd for preparation.**380**

Messenger. So please you, it is true: our thane is coming:
One of my fellows had the speed of him,
Who, almost dead for breath, had scarcely more
Than would make up his message.

Lady Macbeth. Give him tending; **385**
He brings great news.
[Exit Messenger]

The raven himself is hoarse
That croaks the fatal entrance of Duncan
Under my battlements. Come, you spirits **390**
That tend on mortal thoughts, unsex me here,
And fill me from the crown to the toe top-full
Of direst cruelty! make thick my blood;
Stop up the access and passage to remorse,
That no compunctious visitings of nature **395**
Shake my fell purpose, nor keep peace between
The effect and it! Come to my woman's breasts,
And take my milk for gall, you murdering ministers,
Wherever in your sightless substances
You wait on nature's mischief! Come, thick night, **400**
And pall thee in the dunnest smoke of hell,
That my keen knife see not the wound it makes,
Nor heaven peep through the blanket of the dark,
To cry 'Hold, hold!'
[Enter MACBETH] **405**

Great Glamis! worthy Cawdor!
Greater than both, by the all-hail hereafter!
Thy letters have transported me beyond
This ignorant present, and I feel now
The future in the instant.**410**

Macbeth. My dearest love,
Duncan comes here to-night.

Lady Macbeth. And when goes hence?

Macbeth. To-morrow, as he purposes.

Lady Macbeth. O, never **415**
Shall sun that morrow see!
Your face, my thane, is as a book where men
May read strange matters. To beguile the time,
Look like the time; bear welcome in your eye,
Your hand, your tongue: look like the innocent flower, **420**
But be the serpent under't. He that's coming
Must be provided for: and you shall put
This night's great business into my dispatch;
Which shall to all our nights and days to come
Give solely sovereign sway and masterdom.**425**

Macbeth. We **will** speak **fur**ther. (6 **syllables**)

Lady Macbeth. Only **look** up **clear**; (4 **syllables** – a partnership)
To **alter** favour **ever** **is** to **fear**: (10 **syllables**)
Leave **all** the **rest** to **me**. (6 **syllables** – partnership broken)

[Exeunt]

Key Question

How far does Lady Macbeth manipulate her husband?

Grade 6

The conventional **interpretation** of this moment is it reveals Macbeth's love for his wife, whom he calls "my dearest partner of greatness". This is a marriage of mutual support. Perhaps we can also read into it Macbeth's worry that Lady Macbeth is grief stricken, following the death of their child. So, he wants to bring her "good" news which will do her good. He wants to change her mood to one of "rejoicing". The idea that "greatness is promised thee" suggests that it will give her renewed hope in the marriage.

This love then contributes to his **hamartia**. Lady Macbeth's ambition is more **powerful** than his own, so she is able to **manipulate** him by asking him to prove his "love".

The speed with which she comes up with a plan to commit *regicide* is an indication of her true evil nature. This is reinforced by her shocking rejection of her female **role** in a **patriarchal society**, and even more by her shocking rejection of **Christian morality**.

Firstly, she rejects her husband's "milk of human kindness". Then she rejects her own **feminine** nature, asking to be made full of "direst cruelty" **because** she sees this as a **masculine characteristic**. Secondly, she calls on "murdering ministers" and "spirits", turning to the **supernatural** and rejecting God.

Macbeth is nearly speechless, and has little to say. He wants to "speak further", but Lady Macbeth virtually dismisses this. She takes control, making sure she has the last word, "leave all the rest to me". This challenge to Macbeth's authority is also shocking to a *Jacobean* **audience** who would demand **subservience** from a wife. Her rejection of **society**'s expectation of women is almost as evil, from their **perspective**, as turning to the **supernatural**.

What are the 3 main ideas you want to remember so far?

1._____

_____

2._____

_____

3._____

_____

Grade 7

However Shakespeare also wants us to fully understand the **psychology** of both Macbeth and Lady Macbeth. He could so easily have begun with Macbeth telling his wife the weird sisters' prophecies, and she could have then begun to try to persuade him towards *regicide*. This is all the **plot** needs. So, let's understand why **Shakespeare** rejects that, and what it is he wants us to understand about the **characters'** **motivation**s.

> This have I thought good to deliver
> thee, my dearest partner of greatness, that thou **355**
> mightst not lose the dues of rejoicing, by being
> ignorant of what greatness is promised thee.

The first question is why he sends the letter. If it is simply to deliver "good" news, why does he preface it with, "This have I thought good to deliver / Thee"? This rather suggests he has weighed up the consequence of sending the letter. He must have had doubts about doing so, which suggests he knows she is likely to think about *regicide*. The letter is now intended to allow Lady Macbeth to think about "what greatness is promised thee" so she can shape her future.

Firstly, Macbeth **empathises** with his wife as a woman. In *Jacobean* **society**, a woman cannot shape her own destiny except through marriage. There are no other **role**s open to her. Macbeth's **language** also rejects this **patriarchal view** of women, calling her "my dearest partner of greatness". He tells her he sees her as nearly his equal, a "partner" in the "greatness" of becoming queen. This flattery invites Lady Macbeth to come up with a plan to kill Duncan. Why else send the letter?

As Macbeth observes later, "I have no spur to prick the sides of my intent." He is disappointed to realise he has settled on allowing **fate** to make him king whenever **fate** is ready. **Therefore** he wants Lady Macbeth to be that "spur", so he can become king quickly.

Grade 8

The letter is also written in **prose**, so that the **rhythm** is not always **iambic**, and the lines exceed 10 **syllables**. **Shakespeare** normally gives **prose** to his **characters** of low **social status**, whereas anyone of noble birth speaks in more refined **iambic pentameter**. This is perhaps a subtle reminder from Macbeth to his wife about her lack of **status**. This only makes sense if the lack of **status** in question is not being queen. So, the **prose** nature of the letter invites her to want to change her **status** quickly, rather than wait for "chance".

Macbeth also refers to her with the familiar, loving **direct address** of "thou" and "thee". But this is also a subtle reminder of her low **status**, to motivate her to want to change it.

Grade 9

Lady Macbeth's reaction suggests that she knows Macbeth cannot bring himself to act against his king, that he is too **moral**.

> yet do I fear thy nature; **360**
> It is too full o' the milk of human kindness
> To catch the nearest way: thou wouldst be great;
> Art not without ambition, but without
> The illness should attend it:

She believes he is "too full o'the milk of human kindness" as a **metaphor** for his **moral** conscience. **However**, she also has in mind a mother's milk. Here she **characterises** Macbeth as essentially **feminine**, lactating kindness like a mother feeding her baby. We will see how she keeps insulting him by focusing on his **feminine** "nature" once they meet. She sees this as so wrong in a man and a husband that her line is also wrong, breaking the **pentameter** at a full 12 **syllables** long.

As we have seen, **Shakespeare constructs** Lady Macbeth as a terrible figure, who deserves to be punished for becoming **masculine** and pursuing action and "ambition" like a man. **Consequently**, in order to become more **powerful** (and **therefore** rejecting the *Jacobean* **view** of women as **subservient** to men), he makes her call on the **supernatural** "spirits" as servants. A modern **audience** reads "tend on mortal thoughts" as indicating that the evil spirits are drawn to her evil nature, and **therefore** influence her to become more shockingly evil. Many critics even ask if Lady Macbeth is like a fourth witch.

But a *Jacobean* meaning of "tend on", means 'attend on or to'. In other words, the **supernatural** does not influence the "human", it is the other way around. The **supernatural** is **power**less until invited in. To *Jacobeans*, this is proof that she is more evil than Macbeth, **because** he did not invite the witches to influence him.

It is very easy to read this as a logical extension of *Original sin*, where Eve's temptation to ignore God's law is seen as worse than Adam's, **because** she gave in to Satan, whereas Adam gave in only to her. *Original sin* is **therefore** also a **Christian** doctrine that supports the **patriarchal view** of women. They simply deserve to be **inferior**, **because** God says they are, **because** of Eve's *Original sin* and temptation of Adam.

What are the 3 main ideas you want to remember so far?

1._____

_____

3._____

_____

4._____

_____

Beyond Grade 9

However, let's consider an **alternative**, that **Shakespeare** is critical of this **role** given to women in **patriarchal** *Jacobean* England.

What prompts Lady Macbeth is not just evil, it is how her whole **status** in **society** depends on her husband and her **role** as mother. If Macbeth is insecure **because** he has had to fight for **status**, then her **status** is just as insecure. Indeed, Macbeth's warrior nature is what has marked him out as a good husband, as he has literally fought and killed to gain his titles. This is why **society** makes her reject his "human kindness", as it doesn't lead to **social status,** and in fact will hinder him from reaching it.

Her other **role** is to have children and, in a noble family of a thane, to provide heirs. She has failed in this. Not only has she provided no sons, she has provided no living children. This need to provide male heirs has arguably torn English **society** apart. For many, Henry VIII was still part of living memory. In many respects, the persecution of the Catholic church and the creation of a Protestant church of England resulted from Henry's inability to father sons. It certainly led to the murder and divorce of several wives. If Henry's first wife had given birth to sons, he would not have needed to divorce her, to challenge the Catholic church, or destroy the monasteries.

Similarly, in this **society**, only a generation ago, even queens were disposable commodities. We can clearly **infer** that this was an overwhelming factor in Henry's daughter, Elizabeth 1st refusing to marry, and give up her authority. As queen, she had absolute **power**, but as a wife of a king, she would be **subservient** to her husband.

So Lady Macbeth clearly sees herself as similarly disposable. She has given birth, but the child has died very recently, as she is still lactating. Not only does she suffer the terrible grief of a mother who has lost her child, she has also lost all that this stands for – her **status** in **society** and also in her own marriage.

It is no surprise that she **interpret**s men, and **masculinity**, as essentially cruel. This is why, to become a successful man, she asks to be filled with "direst cruelty." She also assumes that, as the king is **superior** to all other men, he must also be so much crueller than other men. We can **infer** this from her **metaphor**, "fill me from the crown". Her primary meaning is from the top of her head, but the choice of "crown" signals how she thinks that kings themselves must be spectacularly cruel.

Shakespeare perhaps has an **alternative motive** here. His play creates a cruel king and queen, and then delivers them a **tragic** end. In this way, he is reaching out to King James and teaching him a lesson in good kingship and wise rule, to avoid cruelty.

Meanwhile, it is **traditional**for directors to decide that Lady Macbeth seduces Macbeth when he arrives, and that she presents the killing of Duncan as a kind of crime of passion, partly to prove his love for his wife, and so treat her as his "partner of greatness." **However**, her invocation to "Come to my woman's breasts, / And take my milk for gall, you murdering ministers" does not present her as a seductress. Her breasts represent motherhood and fertility, which she now completely rejects, asking for her breast milk to be turned to poison, "gall".

Summarise this in one brilliant sentence.

_____

_____

_____

_____

_____

This violent **image** suggests that her mind is affected by terrible grief at the recent death of her baby. She also refuses to be defined by motherhood. She doesn't just want to be queen, she wants equal **status** to a man.

This is exactly the same **psychology** as Elizabeth First who had died only three years before, and was widely admired as an excellent ruler. **Shakespeare portrays** women as **powerful** in their own right, through Lady Macbeth. But he also shows how **society** refuses them that **power**, again through Lady Macbeths exclusion from **power** once she becomes queen.

Her road to madness begins at this moment. We may argue that **Shakespeare** has the same **patriarchal** prejudice against women as his **society**. **Consequently**, giving up on her God-given **role** as a mother leads to her punishment with guilt and madness.

However, to those who see **Shakespeare** as critical of his **patriarchal society**, her guilt and madness are caused by the impossible position she finds herself in. Her route to equal **power** depends on her imitating the stereotype of the soldier, embracing the warrior **culture** that defines her husband, and seeking "direst cruelty" like Macbeth's persona in battle.

Shakespeare next links her to Eve. In support of the **patriarchy**, he gives her these words to teach Macbeth how to deceive: "look like the innocent flower, **/** But be the serpent under't." In this **interpretation**, she shapes her husband's downfall by tempting him with *regicide*. The **reference** to "the serpent" is a clear **allusion** to **Genesis** and Satan, so a *Jacobean* audience can again criticise her as a sinful temptress.

However, an **alternative interpretation** is that **Shakespeare** wants us to focus on her lack of **power** in a **patriarchal society**. This sexism has led to her desperate desire to become queen. This is why she **portrays** Macbeth as looking like "the innocent flower", a deliberately **feminine simile**. This suggests that Macbeth has to become more **feminine** in order for Lady Macbeth to become more **masculine**. She **therefore** follows it with this instruction, "Only look up clear; / To alter favour ever is to fear: / Leave all the rest to me."

Here she points out that Macbeth has too many **feminine** qualities already – he is likely to show "fear" and he is likely to have a muddled mind, rather than "look up clear." In some ways she emasculates him, asking him to take the **subservient** and **feminine role** in the marriage, while she both plans and carries out the murder, "Leave all the rest to me." The **iambic pentameter emphasises** "all", which again suggests that she is more capable than her husband. She thinks she will need no help from him at all, other than to look "innocent". This is also reflected in her 6 **syllable** line. Macbeth should respond with 4 more to fit the **pentameter**, but she has silenced him, and taken charge.

It is interesting to wonder how Macbeth would react to her if she had been able to carry out this plan and murder Duncan herself. He appears happy to let her carry out the assassination. But when she doesn't follow through on her own plan, he begins to lose trust in her, and stops confiding his plans in her. We might argue that Macbeth would survive the murder of Duncan, **because** everyone blames Malcolm and Donalbain. It is only when he has Banquo murdered, and then sees Banquo's ghost in front of the thanes, that his **tragedy** unfolds. Only then does everyone suspect he has murdered Duncan, and only then do they start think about rebelling against his rule.

Summarise this in one brilliant sentence.

_____

_____

_____

What are the 3 main ideas you want to remember so far?

1._____

_____

2._____

_____

3._____

_____

Draw an image in 30 seconds which will help you remember the main ideas.

Label it with 6 key words.

Write 3 sentences. The first words of each one must be in this order. BECAUSE, BUT, SO.

_____

_____

_____

_____

_____

_____

_____

_____

Macbeth's castle.

[Hautboys and torches. Enter a Sewer, and divers] [p]Servants with dishes and service, and pass over the stage. Then enter MACBETH]

Macbeth. If it were done when 'tis done, then 'twere well
It were done quickly: if the assassination **475**
Could trammel up the consequence, and catch
With his surcease success; that but this blow
Might be the be-all and the end-all here,
But here, upon this bank and shoal of time,
We'ld jump the life to come. But in these cases **480**
We still have judgment here; that we but teach
Bloody instructions, which, being taught, return
To plague the inventor: this even-handed justice
Commends the ingredients of our poison'd chalice
To our own lips. He's here in double trust; **485**
First, as I am his kinsman and his subject,
Strong both against the deed; then, as his host,
Who should against his murderer shut the door,
Not bear the knife myself. Besides, this Duncan
Hath borne his faculties so meek, hath been **490**
So clear in his great office, that his virtues
Will plead like angels, trumpet-tongued, against
The deep damnation of his taking-off;
And pity, like a naked new-born babe,
Striding the blast, or heaven's cherubim, horsed **495**
Upon the sightless couriers of the air,
Shall blow the horrid deed in every eye,
That tears shall drown the wind. I have no spur
To prick the sides of my intent, but only
Vaulting ambition, which o'erleaps itself **500**
And falls on the other.
[Enter LADY MACBETH]
How now! what news?

Lady Macbeth. He has almost supp'd: why have you left the chamber?

Macbeth. Hath he ask'd for me?**505**

Lady Macbeth. Know you not he has?

Macbeth. We will proceed no further in this business:
He hath honour'd me of late; and I have bought
Golden opinions from all sorts of people,
Which would be worn now in their newest gloss, **510**
Not cast aside so soon.

Lady Macbeth. Was the hope drunk
Wherein you dress'd yourself? hath it slept since?
And wakes it now, to look so green and pale
At what it did so freely? From this time **515**
Such I account thy love. Art thou afeard
To be the same in thine own act and valour
As thou art in desire? Wouldst thou have that
Which thou esteem'st the ornament of life,
And live a coward in thine own esteem, **520**
Letting 'I dare not' wait upon 'I would,'
Like the poor cat i' the adage?

Macbeth. Prithee, peace:
I dare do all that may become a man;
Who dares do more is none.**525**

Lady Macbeth. What beast was't, then,
That made you break this enterprise to me?
When you durst do it, then you were a man;
And, to be more than what you were, you would
Be so much more the man. Nor time nor place **530**
Did then adhere, and yet you would make both:
They have made themselves, and that their fitness now
Does unmake you. I have given suck, and know
How tender 'tis to love the babe that milks me:
I would, while it was smiling in my face, **535**
Have pluck'd my nipple from his boneless gums,
And dash'd the brains out, had I so sworn as you
Have done to this.

Macbeth. If we should fail?

Lady Macbeth. We fail! **540**
But screw your courage to the sticking-place,
And we'll not fail. When Duncan is asleep—
Whereto the rather shall his day's hard journey
Soundly invite him—his two chamberlains
Will I with wine and wassail so convince **545**
That memory, the warder of the brain,
Shall be a fume, and the receipt of reason
A limbeck only: when in swinish sleep
Their drenched natures lie as in a death,
What cannot you and I perform upon **550**
The unguarded Duncan? what not put upon
His spongy officers, who shall bear the guilt
Of our great quell?

Macbeth. Bring forth men-children only;
For thy undaunted mettle should compose **555**
Nothing but males. Will it not be received,
When we have mark'd with blood those sleepy two

Of his own chamber and used their very daggers,
That they have done't?

Lady Macbeth. Who dares receive it other, **560**
As we shall make our griefs and clamour roar
Upon his death?

Macbeth. I am settled, and bend up
Each corporal agent to this terrible feat.
Away, and mock the time with fairest show: **565**
False face must hide what the false heart doth know.*[Exeunt]*

Key Question

What motivates Macbeth and Lady Macbeth to kill Duncan?

Grade 6

In Macbeth's **soliloquy,** the length of the sentences, the many changes of direction of thought, all suggest that he does not really want to carry through with the murder. But, we must zoom in on the most revealing quotations. Macbeth knows he is going against God and it is a main reason he has for not killing Duncan. This is why he imagines "heaven's cherubim" reacting to Duncan's death. He knows the whole world will see this as a crime against the *Great Chain of Being*, against God and against nature, so he imagines a "horrid deed" stuck "in every eye".

Lady Macbeth uses her evil **power** of **manipulation** to get him to turn away from his doubts. She knows he wants a "spur to prick the sides of [his] intent", and she knows exactly how to be that "spur". Firstly, she attacks his lack of "love", with "such I account thy love", implying his love is insincere and worthless. Then she immediately focuses on his fear, demanding "art thou afeard?"

Finally, she uses the violent **imagery** of killing her own child, claiming she would have "dash'd the brains out" of her own child if she had promised to do this, no matter how painful such a murder should be.

Grade 7

An often overlooked fact is that the Macbeth's have just lost their only child. His grief might well explain his reckless abandon we saw in battle. Now, his dead baby appears to trigger a connection with the death of Duncan, who is innocent. This prompts Macbeth to **personify** "pity" in the form of "a naked new-born babe" reaching "every eye" in Scotland. He imagines the whole population will feel the same grief, in losing their king, as he himself has felt in the death of his baby.

Obviously, this is a rational argument for not killing Duncan. He can **empathise** with how much grief each citizen would feel, and this is a strong reason not to commit *regicide*. But the emotional argument might be different. His pain might be so great that he feels the only way to cope with it is to share it with everyone else, by making them experience what he feels.

Grade 8

There is also a hint of anger at God here for the death of his baby. In his **metaphor**, God sends his own baby angels, "heaven's cherubim" on "sightless couriers." "Sightless" seems to accuse God of being blind, or indifferent, to the pain he has caused Macbeth and Lady Macbeth.

In the next line he refers to the *regicide* as "the horrid deed." Refusing to name it makes the murder more acceptable. There is a suggestion that the murder is a revenge attack against God. The *Great Chain of Being* suggests that the king is appointed by God, and to kill the king is a direct attack on God. We might look at this thought process and realise that this contributes to Macbeth's **motive** in killing Duncan. He is **motivated** by much more than ambition. He welcomes the opportunity to attack God.

> **What are the 3 main ideas you want to remember so far?**
>
> 1._____
>
> _____
>
> 2._____
>
> _____
>
> 3._____
>
> _____

Grade 9

He also **emphasises** one of his most **powerful** reasons for not killing Duncan by keeping it till last, that he is Duncan's "host". In **Greek tragedy**, harming a guest was much more sinful than even killing your own family. Hercules was punished with 12 labours when he killed his wife and children. While Tantalus abused Zeus's hospitality, and was punished for eternity. The importance of hospitality is also highlighted in the Bible, through the stories of Abraham. Just as in **Greek mythology**, God appears to him as a stranger and receives immediate hospitality. The link between Macbeth's guest, Duncan, and God is **therefore** very clear to **Shakespeare**'s educated, *Jacobean* **audience** of nobles.

This **allusion** suggests that Macbeth already knows he will not get away with killing Duncan, that the consequences will be too great. But he still embraces the **role** of **tragic hero**. Why? One reason could be to challenge God. Perhaps more **powerful** one is to reward or comfort Lady Macbeth.

Grade 8

His next thought is to doubt his own resilience and determination to murder Duncan. He uses another **metaphor**, "I have no spur / To prick the sides of my intent, but only / Vaulting ambition".

Firstly, he realises that "ambition" is not enough of a **motive** to make him kill the king. This points to his **hamartia** not being ambition and, as we saw earlier, bloodlust itself is a **powerful** **motive**. In this *scene*, we have also seen he is **motivated** by grief, and anger at the injustice of his baby's death. He believes that if he only relies on "ambition", he won't have enough of a "spur" to carry out his "intent" of killing Duncan, but will in fact fail, falling "on the other" side of the vault, like a horse. We can also see this failure when **Shakespeare**'s makes this line 11 **syllables**, disrupting the **pentameter**.

However, Macbeth's **analogy** of himself as a horse introduces the **image** of a rider providing the spur. We can see that he is depending on Lady Macbeth to be that rider, to take control. It also suggests that his desire to be king is to make her queen, his "dearest partner in greatness". This desire to please her is so **powerful**, he'll do it despite the inevitable "fall". **Therefore** he knows, from the outset, that committing *regicide* will lead to failure. But he is prepared to do it anyway.

She reacts by spurring him on in three ways. First, she appeals to his desire to prove his love to her, appealing to his obvious love for her, "From this time **/** Such I account thy love." The second is to emasculate him further, by accusing him of being afraid: "Art thou afeard / To be the same in thine own act and valour / As thou art in desire?"

Grade 9

We know from the sergeant's report that Macbeth has fought without fear – he is even reckless in the face of danger. Yet, in this warrior **culture**, showing any sign of fear might be the ultimate weakness. **Although** to our modern ear, accusing him of cowardice might seem illogical, and certainly less persuasive than focusing on his love for her, **Shakespeare**'s **society** is different. "Love" is a weaker argument, **because** it involves a woman. Bravery is a stronger argument, **because** it involves only men.

However, the most **powerful** argument, the one which persuades him again to consider killing Duncan, is connected to his grief:

> "I have given suck, and know
> How tender 'tis to love the babe that milks me:
> I would, while it was smiling in my face,
> Have pluck'd my nipple from his boneless gums,
> And dash'd the brains out, had I so sworn as you
> Have done to this."

She links the killing to the pain of losing their "babe". She invokes the grief she feels at their child's death, and claims that she would willingly endure it again, rather than break this promise he has made, to kill the king. We have already seen that killing the king is a response to his own grief. Now we can see he believes it will help Lady Macbeth deal with hers.

Lady Macbeth's words also suggest what a violent **psychological** act she has undertaken in asking to be unsexed, and rejecting motherhood. She has **metaphorical**ly "pluck'd (her) nipple" from all future babies. The violence of her method of killing her own baby, "And dash'd the brains out" also reflects the violence of her grief. Once more, **Shakespeare** gives the line 11 **syllables**, to reflect the excess of grief.

Not fulfilling the **role** of mother is an act of violence against **society**. It suggests that **society** will fight violently against her attempt to gain any semblance of equal **power** or authority, and so Shakespeare has to punish her, first with madness, then suicide.

Beyond Grade 9

One **interpretation** of her suicide is that her **feminine** mind has been overcome by taking on the **masculine characteristic**s of ambition and cruelty, so she is punished for this. **Alternatively**, she knows that if Macbeth is defeated she will simply become another man's property. Rather than become his property, she would rather die.

Macbeth does not share his **patriarchal society**'s **view** of female **inferiority**. His **image** of himself as a horse being ridden by a rider, Lady Macbeth, to "spur" him on also presents her as **masculine**. **Shakespeare** gives her the phallic "prick" instead of 'kick' or 'guide' "the sides of my intent" **because** Macbeth associates Lady Macbeth with **power** and **masculinity**.

Both Lady Macbeth and Macbeth are prepared to die from the outset. Macbeth is finally convinced to kill Duncan when his wife declares that they should not fear failure and death.

> **Macbeth.** If we should fail?
>
> **Lady Macbeth.** We fail!
> But screw your courage to the sticking-place,
> And we'll not fail."

Again, we can see that she partly emasculates him here. She suggests that he does not have enough "courage" in comparison to herself. The repetition of "we" **portrays** their marriage as a partnership, "we'll not fail". So perhaps she is not criticising his lack of **masculinity** here. She is just preserving a balance in the marriage where he has taken on more **feminine** qualities while she has taken on more **masculine** ones.

A **patriarchal viewpoint** at the time, **however**, would see this as an attack on Macbeth's **status** as a male, and add to the need for her punishment. She has also become much more like her husband in battle, who fought "disdaining fortune". Her reply to Macbeth's fear of failure is "We fail!" A life risked taking action is better than passive waiting. We can see this as both of them being seduced by the prize of ambition. But we can also see it as a desperation to flee the present and "to jump the life to come". The **emphasis** isn't on ambition itself. "The life to come", the **fate**d kingship that weird sisters promised, is inevitable.

The attraction is "to jump", to seek action. On the one hand this desire is caused by their intense grief at the death of their only child. On the other, it fits the **psychology** of the bloodthirsty warrior and the socially oppressed wife who wants, more than anything, to take charge of her own destiny as "partner" rather than be tied to a man. This is why her response is only two words long, and it begins with their partnership, "We".

Shakespeare structures their shared lines to **emphasise** this partnership, as though he wants us to realise that Lady Macbeth is not just **motivated** by ambition, but much more by changing **social** conventions, demanding an equal **role** in the **patriarchy**. The **iambic** meter is **consequently** shared between them:

> "**Lady Macbeth.** …Have *done* to *this*.
>
> **Macbeth.** If *we* should *fail*?
>
> **Lady Macbeth.** We *fail*!"

The **iambic rhythm** forces the **stress** on the words in bold italics. Notice that **Shakespeare** gives Macbeth the **emphasise**d "we". This suggests that he sees their marriage as a partnership, and wishes to challenge **social** convention by championing his wife's **power**.

She in fact points this out at the beginning of his doubts, "What beast was't, then, / That made you break this enterprise to me?" Some commentators **interpret** this to mean that Macbeth has discussed killing Duncan before the play started, but this hardly fits with Macbeth's horror when he first reacts to the weird sisters' prophecies. Instead, she lets him know that she understands exactly why he wrote to her about those prophesies – it was an invitation to her to start plotting *regicide*.

At this stage it appears that Macbeth has total trust in his wife, and she fully intends to kill Duncan at her husband's side. There are two daggers, belonging to the two grooms, and she intends for them to use one each: "What cannot you and I perform upon / The unguarded Duncan?"

She knows the violence of the murder will appeal to Macbeth's bloodlust. After all, a sleeping man is efficiently killed with one stroke of the dagger. But Lady Macbeth wants Macbeth to imagine a much greater brutality which will require two of them to "perform upon" the king.

Because she knows her **manipulation** is working, she changes the **personal pronoun**. Now she addresses him with respect, as "you". **Shakespeare**'s **audience** would notice this change from "thy love" and "Art thou afeard". Her use of the in**formal** pronoun suggested both intimacy and Macbeth's decline in **status** in her eyes.

Write 3 sentences. Use the words highlighted in the notes (as these are subject terminology).

_____

_____

_____

_____

_____

_____

_____

A Note About Time

It is worth noting that time is very much compressed in this play. It is possible for the battle to take place over the course of the day, then for Macbeth and Banquo to meet Duncan on another day, and then for them all to arrive at Macbeth's castle on a later day. In real time, this is exactly what would happen.

But **Shakespeare** gives us a few hints that this natural unfolding of time doesn't occur in the play. Firstly, he is a writing a **tragedy**, and borrowing from the **Greek** tradition, set out by Aristotle in Ars **Poetic**a. This means that he wants to compress time. In the unity of time actually states that all the action should take place over a 24 hour day.

Secondly, the sergeant's arrival to give an account to Duncan, before seeing a surgeon for his bleeding wounds, proves that the king's camp is very close to the battle, he is at "A camp near Forres", where his castle is.

It is very possible, even in real time, that this battle could commence just before dawn and end in the early morning. Ross intercepts Macbeth close by, on "A heath near Forres" to tell him he is now thane of Cawdor. Macbeth and Banquo join the king at Forres, where they receive news of Malcolm's position as heir. Then Duncan finishes the *scene* saying, "Let's after him, / Whose care is gone before to bid us welcome."

This clearly points to Macbeth returning at once to Inverness, and Duncan following quickly "after him."

Summarise this in one brilliant sentence.

_____

_____

_____

_____

_____

A Vital Note on Staging

This allows the actor playing Macbeth to arrive still covered in blood from battle, and creates a visual **symbol** of his bloodlust when he greets Lady Macbeth. It also forces us to look again at the letter he sends his wife – if he really is arriving that same day, then the *only* reason for the letter is to encourage Lady Macbeth to begin planning *regicide*.

True, a director does have time to take Macbeth out of his bloody clothes. During Lady Macbeth's **soliloquys** as she reads his letter. This will allow us not to have time as compressed, and to imagine some days have passed since the battle. So we could argue that **Shakespeare** does not intend to have Macbeth arrive in a bloody state.

However, I think the next *scene* proves Macbeth does arrive bloody from battle. Act I *scene* 6 shows Duncan's arrival where he is greeted by Lady Macbeth, and *Macbeth is absent.* This would be an extraordinary lapse in etiquette, and Duncan **allude**s to this by telling her "conduct me to mine host". The logistical reason for Macbeth's absence in performance has to be that the actor needs to change clothes for the banquet. So he must have arrived in blood spattered battle armour.

This clothes change will also help **emphasise** the "robes" he will be wearing as thane of Cawdor, the ones he tells his wife he should enjoy in their "newest gloss".

Pay attention to this, **because** it is going to be crucial later that night when Banquo says "I dreamt last night of the three weird sisters." "Last night" will be the night *before* the battle and *before* they meet the witches. It will suggest either that he is lying, or that the witches have tried to **manipulate** Banquo, before they **manipulate**d Macbeth.

A Note on Thou and You

Shakespeare's **audience** were very attuned to **social status**. Just like the French in**formal** 'tu' and **formal** 'vous', and the Spanish 'tu' and 'usted', English _Jacobeans_ also had the **formal** and in**formal** versions of this **personal pronoun**.

'You' was **formal**, used with **social superior**s, and to show neutral feelings.

'Thou' was in**formal**, and used to convey closeness, friendship or love. **However**, it also conveyed the **status** of the speaker – a **social superior** would use 'thou' to show that they did not need to show respect for the listener's **status**. In these circumstances, the listener would still have to reply with 'you', not 'thou'.

This is really relevant here **because** of the way Lady Macbeth's **language** has had to change. She begins the _scene_ addressing him **formal**ly, as "you" deferring to his higher **social status because** he is her husband.

You might also notice how often she reinforces that **status** in the play when she calls him "lord" or "thane". **However**, when she feels he has betrayed her love, she immediately changes to the in**formal** "thou":

> "From this time
> Such I account thy love. Art thou afeard
> To be the same in thine own act and valour
> As thou art in desire?"

This **emphasises** the love she feels he should demonstrate to her and for her. It also indicates her loss of respect for him, as he is no longer deserving of being addressed as 'you'.

She addresses him again **formal**ly as "you" when she speaks of his strength, rather than his weakness: "When you durst do it, then you were a man". This implies that he is only manly when he acts out of bravery and out of love. This is the only way for him to gain the respect he deserves, and his **status**.

Build Long Term Memory!

Draw an image in 30 seconds which will help you remember the main ideas.

Label it with 6 key words.

Write 3 sentences. Use the words highlighted in the notes (as these are subject terminology).

_____

_____

_____

_____

_____

_____

_____

_____

Revise Act 1

Use the next page to summarise what you have learned during Act 1. You might:

1. Draw a mind map, using the pictures you have already used in your notes.
2. Present your learning in columns, focusing on 5 key quotations.
3. Something you prefer.

Quote	Terminology	Beautiful sentence	Context	Shakespeare's purpose	Alternative interpretation	Link to other part of the play

Act II, *Scene* 1

Court of Macbeth's castle

[Enter BANQUO, and FLEANCE bearing a torch before him]

Banquo. How goes the night, boy?

Fleance. The moon is down; I have not heard the clock.**570**

Banquo. And she goes down at twelve.

Fleance. I take't, 'tis later, sir.

Banquo. Hold, take my sword. There's husbandry in heaven;
Their candles are all out. Take thee that too.
A heavy summons lies like lead upon me, **575**
And yet I would not sleep: merciful **power**s,
Restrain in me the cursed thoughts that nature
Gives way to in repose!

[Enter MACBETH, and a Servant with a torch]

Give me my sword. **580**
Who's there?

Macbeth. A friend.

Banquo. What, sir, not yet at rest? The king's a-bed:
He hath been in unusual pleasure, and
Sent forth great largess to your offices. **585**
This diamond he greets your wife withal,
By the name of most kind hostess; and shut up
In measureless content.

Macbeth. Being unprepared,
Our will became the servant to defect; **590**
Which else should free have wrought.

Banquo. All's well.
I dreamt last night of the three weird sisters:
To you they have show'd some truth. (7 **syllables**)

Macbeth. I think not of them: **595** (5 **syllables** – not in agreement)
Yet, when we can entreat an hour to serve,
We would spend it in some words upon that business,
If you would grant the time.

Banquo. At your kind'st leisure.

Macbeth. If you shall cleave to my consent, when 'tis, **600**
It shall make honour for you.

Banquo. So I lose none
In seeking to augment it, but still keep
My bosom franchised and allegiance clear,
I shall be counsell'd.**605**

Macbeth. Good repose the while!

Banquo. Thanks, sir: the like to you!

[Exeunt BANQUO and FLEANCE]

Macbeth. Go bid thy mistress, when my drink is ready,
She strike upon the bell. Get thee to bed. **610**
[Exit Servant]

Is this a dagger which I see before me,
The handle toward my hand? Come, let me clutch thee.
I have thee not, and yet I see thee still.
Art thou not, fatal vision, sensible **615**
To feeling as to sight? or art thou but
A dagger of the mind, a false creation,
Proceeding from the heat-oppressed brain?
I see thee yet, in form as palpable
As this which now I draw. **620**
Thou marshall'st me the way that I was going;
And such an instrument I was to use.
Mine eyes are made the fools o' the other senses,
Or else worth all the rest; I see thee still,
And on thy blade and dudgeon gouts of blood, **625**
Which was not so before. There's no such thing:
It is the bloody business which informs
Thus to mine eyes. Now o'er the one halfworld
Nature seems dead, and wicked dreams abuse
The curtain'd sleep; witchcraft celebrates **630**
Pale Hecate's offerings, and wither'd murder,
Alarum'd by his sentinel, the wolf,
Whose howl's his watch, thus with his stealthy pace.
With Tarquin's ravishing strides, towards his design
Moves like a ghost. Thou sure and firm-set earth, **635**
Hear not my steps, which way they walk, for fear
Thy very stones prate of my whereabout,
And take the present horror from the time,
Which now suits with it. Whiles I threat, he lives:
Words to the heat of deeds too cold breath gives. **640**
[A bell rings]

I go, and it is done; the bell invites me.
Hear it not, Duncan; for it is a knell
That summons thee to heaven or to hell.

[Exit]

Key Question

Why do Shakespeare and Macbeth decide that Banquo won't help kill Duncan, but that instead Macbeth will also kill Banquo?

Grade 6

This *scene* presents us with our greatest insight into Banquo's mind. As we have already seen, Banquo was believed to be King James's ancestor, so he had to be presented as noble. **However**, **because** Shakespeare was interested in **motivation** and **psychology**, he presented Banquo as wrestling with his desires.

> "A heavy summons lies like lead upon me,
> And yet I would not sleep: merciful **power**s,
> Restrain in me the cursed thoughts that nature
> Gives way to in repose!"

The "cursed thoughts" suggest that he is being tempted to help Macbeth kill Duncan, so that the prophecies can begin to come true. Or it suggests he is worried that Macbeth will kill Duncan, and he ought to try to prevent this. He tries to get Macbeth to discuss his plans by claiming "I dreamt last night of the three weird sisters." This could be **because** he wants to talk about a partnership in helping Macbeth become king, like the real, **historical** Banquo did. Or it could be **because** he wants to dissuade Macbeth from *regicide*, so he needs Macbeth to discuss the prophecies with him.

Grade 7

But, what is the "summons"? It could be God, urging him to stop Macbeth's plan to kill Duncan. But the **simile** "like lead" suggests that this is a heavy weight which is dragging him down, **because** he doesn't want to do it. He actually needs Macbeth to become king if Fleance is going to follow him as king. "Lead" is also **symbolic** of a base metal in **Shakespeare**'s England, and **therefore** indicates a base, or evil desire. He points out that he is having "cursed thoughts", as though the weird sisters have cursed him by giving him this knowledge of the future. So, one possibility is that he is thinking about letting Macbeth kill Duncan. A further possibility is that he is actually thinking about helping Macbeth to kill Duncan.

This is of course what happened **historical**ly. **Shakespeare**'s source, Holinshed's Chronicles makes this clear. So, **Shakespeare** rewrote history by making Banquo refuse his own "nature" to kill Duncan and bring his son's destiny as future king closer. This makes Banquo's decision not to give in to this temptation both human and noble.

Alternatively, we can read this "summons" as a warning to take care of Fleance, believing that Macbeth is already thinking of killing Fleance. We might read the passing of his "sword" to Fleance as a **symbol** that Banquo is teaching him to defend himself.

> "**Banquo.** All's well.
> I dreamt last night of the three weird sisters:
> To you they have show'd some truth. (7 **syllables**)
>
> **Macbeth.** I think not of them". (5 **syllables**)

Banquo's words cause us a problem. We have already seen how **Shakespeare** has compressed time. For Banquo to have "dreamt last night of the three weird sisters" he would mean that this was a premonition – a dream before they met the witches on the heath.

The **Christian interpretation**, and the one that would appeal to King James, is that this invites Macbeth to consider that the weird sisters are manipulating them both. Macbeth must realise they are affecting Banquo's mind like his own. This would give Banquo time to persuade Macbeth not to act on the prophecies.

Alternatively, perhaps time is not compressed. If he tells Macbeth that he has been thinking about their prophecies today, days after their encounter, it invites Macbeth to wonder if Banquo is also thinking he will help kill Duncan.

Macbeth's reply, "I think not of them" is an obvious lie. He cannot expect Banquo to believe this, given what they prophesied, and given how visibly Macbeth was affected, "rapt withal" when he heard them. Macbeth's lie is essential, as to talk about the witches now, and then find Duncan murdered in the morning, will immediately cause suspicion. But he knows Banquo will know it is a lie, and **consequently** Banquo becomes a threat who, in Macbeth's mind, will have to be assassinated.

What are the 3 main ideas you want to remember so far?

1._____

_____

2._____

_____

3._____

_____

Grade 9

Shakespeare disrupts the **iambic pentameter** to signal that both men are lying. Banquo's "***the*** three ***weird sisters***" cannot really be spoken with **iambic stresses**, as I've shown here in bold. "**The three weird**" must all be **stress ed**, which conveys how important they are as well as how hard Banquo is having to work in his lie. This effort leads to him losing control of the **pentameter**. This is further evidence that time has been compressed, and he didn't dream of them.

Macbeth's "**I think not of them**" feels **trochaic**, as he **stresses** the first **syllable**. **However**, his words continue Banquo's previous line, following in his **iambic stresses**. But, in trying to follow on harmoniously from Banquo's words, **Shakespeare** signals how hard Macbeth is working in his lie, so that their combined line has twelve **syllables**.

This is **therefore** the turning point in their relationship, with each man lying to the other. In many ways it is much more important than Macbeth's **soliloquy** listing all the reasons not to kill Duncan. His murder of Duncan leads to temporary guilt. But his killing of Banquo leads to prolonged haunting.

The two men never get beyond this stalemate **because** Banquo insists on keeping his "conscience clear", and Macbeth realises he cannot count on Banquo as an ally. From this moment, then, he decides that he will also have to kill Banquo.

Obviously, **Shakespeare** changes Banquo's **historical role** as an accomplice in *regicide* to flatter King James about his ancestor. But more importantly, **Shakespeare** needs to teach the nobles attending his performance that *regicide* can only lead to **tragedy**. In **historical** fact, Macbeth was not threatened by Banquo and reigned for 20 years, a significant term. *Regicide* was clearly a great success!

Summarise this in one brilliant sentence.

_____

_____

_____

_____

_____

Grade 6

When Macbeth is left on his own, **Shakespeare** shows the personal cost of his decision to kill Duncan by the hallucination of the dagger.

> "Is this a dagger which I see before me, (11 **syllables**)
> The handle toward my hand? Come, let me clutch thee." (12 **syllables**)

We can see that the dagger is controlling Macbeth. First, it turns its "handle toward" Macbeth's "hand" as though it is inviting him to murder Duncan. Macbeth then asks permission, "let me clutch thee", as though the dagger is making him want to kill Duncan. When he asks if the dagger is "a false creation" and produced by his own "heat oppressed brain" we can see that Macbeth has created it himself in order to help him mentally prepare for *regicide*.

The vision tells us that Macbeth is now no longer in charge of his mental faculties. Some productions decide that the weird sisters have created this vision. To illustrate this, the witches would appear silently on stage, as though manipulating Macbeth with the vision.

However, **Shakespeare** does not push this **interpretation**. For example, Macbeth never asks himself who has put the invisible dagger in front of him. He only supposes it is "a dagger of the mind". This **therefore** suggests that it is the first sign of madness which will affect both Macbeth and Lady Macbeth, ending with her sleepwalking and suicide. **Shakespeare therefore portrays** the act of *regicide* as an act of madness, which will also make the assassin mad. It is obviously propaganda aimed at warning any noble against regicide.

Grade 7

But his mind also warns him not to kill. His vision is "false". Perhaps this means he is not just a traitor to Duncan, but actually false to himself. This sense of his own mind warning him is also **emphasise**d by disrupting the **iambic pentameter** again. Again, he increases the number of **syllables**. The **couplet** has 11 and 12 **syllables** respectively. His most **dramatic** change is to the **iambic stresses**. "Come, let me clutch thee" which is difficult to perform without **stress**ing each **syllable**. This **emphasis** conveys how desperately he wants to hold on to the dagger which will kill Duncan.

Grade 8

It **symbolises** his bloodlust, his desire to kill, much more than his ambition simply to become king. The **alliteration** of "come" and "clutch" also shows a desperation to kill, but also suggests that he wants the dagger, **metaphorical**ly, always in his hand, "clutched" **foreshadows** how addicted to violence he will become in his actions later in the play.

An often missed point is that there is only one dagger in this vision. This was not part of the original plan, where Macbeth and Lady Macbeth would both "perform / On the unguarded Duncan" with two daggers. This might suggest that Macbeth always planned to carry out the murder himself, and he only needed his wife as the "spur" to force him out of his conscience. This would explain why Lady Macbeth tells us that Duncan looked too much like her "father as he slept", but Macbeth never mentions it. He never criticises her for it. It is as though he always expected her to pull out of the actual killing.

Grade 9

The attraction of the murder is also not just in replacing Duncan, it is bloodlust again. Notice how the dagger now changes: "And on thy blade and dudgeon gouts of blood". The ferocity of the killing is also suggested by blood on the "dudgeon", which is the handle of the knife. Macbeth literally wants to get his hands dirty with blood.

What are the 3 main ideas you want to remember so far?

1._____

_____

2._____

_____

3._____

_____

Beyond Grade 9

He also **personifies** "murder" who he imagines "With Tarquin's ravishing strides, towards his design / Moves like a ghost." This is fascinating. Firstly, he has already **reference**d "Hecate", who he imagines has made "offerings" to "witchcraft". Macbeth **therefore** presents witchcraft as separate to this murder. It also distances Macbeth's thoughts from "witchcraft". He has made no such offerings. In his own mind, he is not killing Duncan **because** of the witches' influence.

Instead, he identifies with the "ghost" of "Tarquin". This is an **allusion** to **Shakespeare**'s poem, The Rape of Lucrece. On one level it is a quick advert to potential patrons in the **audience** – there was a lot of money to be gained by writing poems to order. Several times in **Shakespeare**'s career all theatres were shut down to prevent plague outbreaks from spreading. During those months he earned an income through his **poetry**, writing it for various lords. It reminds us that the play is always a way of making money, and in this case pursuing the patronage of King James.

But it also casts Macbeth in a different light. Tarquin is already a king when he commits his crime, so in his mind Macbeth already sees himself as a king, who deserves the crown. He is also a Roman king, who believed in **pagan** gods, and crucially had no concept of hell, or an eternal soul. Evil is not relevant in such a world, but enjoying and keeping **power** is.

Tarquin's son, whose middle name was also Tarquin, raped Lucrecia and she eventually committed suicide **because** of this. This again **portrays** the murder in sexual terms, linking to Macbeth's bloodlust. Macbeth thinks of "murder" in sexual tones, so that Tarquin's movements are "ravishing". It reveals Macbeth's **powerful** attraction to the act of killing, feeding his bloodlust. The fact that he is killing Duncan is of secondary importance to him than his enjoyment of the murder itself.

It might also **allude** to Lady Macbeth's suicide. **Shakespeare contrasts** her suicide, which is caused by her guilt in her crime against the king, to Lucrecia's, which is caused by her innocence and the crimes of the king. This implies her suicide is Macbeth's fault, as he plays the **role** of Tarquin in this metaphor.

Another reason for Macbeth thinking of Tarquin is that the real Tarquin the Proud (Lucius Tarquinius Superbus) was a tyrant who became king **because** his wife, Tullia, persuaded him to assassinate the existing king. A deliberate parallel is that this king Servius was actually his father in law, Tullia's father. Whereas Lady Macbeth does not actually kill Duncan, who looks like her father, Tullia did not kill her own father. But she did ride her chariot over her father's dead body, splattering her clothes with blood. Shakespeare plays with this **image** when Lady Macbeth returns with bloodied hands from Duncan's blood.

This level of detail is highly relevant to **Shakespeare**'s **audience**, who would have had a classical education in **Greek** and Roman history, as well as reading in ancient **Greek** and Latin. They would also know that Tarquin bought three books of *prophecy* from the Cumaen Sybil. This of course adds to the parallel with Macbeth and the three prophecies of the weird sisters.

Shakespeare also has Macbeth turn to pre-**Christian** figures in Hecate and Tarquin. This subtly suggests that Macbeth does not believe in a **Christian** world **view**. This will make it much easier for him to ignore The *Great Chain of Being* as an artificial **Christian construct**, and prevent him worrying about the natural order. This also marks out another element of his **hamartia**, that he does not have a strong enough belief in God.

What are the 2 main ideas you want to remember so far?
1._____   _____   2._____

This will make him much different from Lady Macbeth, who pays far more attention to her soul, and the idea of eternal damnation and hell.

Because his **audience** are deeply **Christian**, **Shakespeare** gives Macbeth a deliberate **Christian reference** as his final words before killing Duncan:

> "I go, and it is done; the bell invites me.
> Hear it not, Duncan; for it is a knell
> That summons thee to heaven or to hell."

The **reference** to "hell" may be a clear **allusion** to Macbeth's **fate**. But **Shakespeare** offers us many more possibilities here. Firstly, Macbeth imagines that Duncan's soul might well end up in "hell", suggesting that he is deserving of this death, and has not been a **moral** man or king.

Secondly, the balancing of the two opposites, "to heaven or to hell" implies that he treats them both equally. This is impossible for a **Christian**, and **therefore** indicates that Macbeth doesn't really believe in either of these. A final way that indicates a lack of **Christian** belief is in over **rhyming**. Normally, the *scene* would end with a simple **rhyming couplet**, but **Shakespeare** adds an internal **rhyme**, "bell…knell…hell." This gives it a childlike tone, almost mocking what he is about to do.

To a **Christian audience**, this shows the terrible sacrilege of Macbeth's act of killing God's appointed king. It also suggests Macbeth's possible atheism. **Shakespeare** also adds the extra **syllable** to this line, where Macbeth speaks in the **passive voice** "the bell invites me". This extra **syllable** perhaps indicates how Macbeth is lying to himself. He thinks the murder will be easy, but in his final words he cannot portray himself carrying out that murder. Instead, it is "the bell" which makes him do it. Of course, "the bell" is rung by his wife, so this is another way in which he decides, **psychological**ly, that it is easier to carry out the murder if it is her idea. This will also allow him, should he feel the need to regret his actions, to blame his wife.

But he also refuses to see himself committing the murder. Instead, "it is done", as though he has not actually committed the murder Duncan himself.

We can **interpret** this as his mind already rebelling against him, refusing to deal with the **psychological** impact of the terrible sin he is committing. Or we can see it as Macbeth's desperation to get it over with, where "done" does not mean "performed" but completed.

Build Long Term Memory!

Write 3 sentences. The first words of each one must be in this order. BECAUSE, BUT, SO.

_____

_____

_____

_____

_____

_____

_____

_____

Draw an image in 30 seconds which will help you remember the main ideas.

Label it with 6 key words.

Go back over this whole section and pick out the top 5 ideas you need to remember.

1._____

_____

2._____

_____

3._____

_____

4._____

_____

5._____

_____

The same.

[Enter LADY MACBETH]

Lady Macbeth. That which hath made them drunk hath made me bold;
What hath quench'd them hath given me fire.
Hark! Peace!
It was the owl that shriek'd, the fatal bellman, **650**
Which gives the stern'st good-night. He is about it:
The doors are open; and the surfeited grooms
Do mock their charge with snores: I have drugg'd
their possets,
That death and nature do contend about them, **655**
Whether they live or die.

Macbeth. *[Within]* Who's there? what, ho!

Lady Macbeth. Alack, I am afraid they have awaked,
And 'tis not done. The attempt and not the deed
Confounds us. Hark! I laid their daggers ready; **660**
He could not miss 'em. Had he not resembled
My father as he slept, I had done't.

[Enter MACBETH]

My husband!

Macbeth. I have done the deed. Didst thou not hear a noise?**665**

Lady Macbeth. I heard the owl scream and the crickets cry.
Did not you speak?

Macbeth. When?

Lady Macbeth. Now.

Macbeth. As I descended?**670**

Lady Macbeth. Ay.

Macbeth. Hark!
Who lies i' the second chamber?

Lady Macbeth. Donalbain.

Macbeth. This is a sorry sight.**675**

[Looking on his hands]

Lady Macbeth. A foolish thought, to say a sorry sight.

Macbeth. There's one did laugh in's sleep, and one cried 'Murder!'
That they did wake each other: I stood and heard them: **680**
But they did say their prayers, and address'd them
Again to sleep.

Lady Macbeth. There are two lodged together.

Macbeth. One cried 'God bless us!' and 'Amen' the other;
As they had seen me with these hangman's hands. **685**
Listening their fear, I could not say 'Amen,'
When they did say 'God bless us!'

Lady Macbeth. Consider it not so deeply.

Macbeth. But wherefore could not I pronounce 'Amen'?
I had most need of blessing, and 'Amen' **690**
Stuck in my throat.

Lady Macbeth. These deeds must not be thought
After these ways; so, it will make us mad.

Macbeth. Methought I heard a voice cry 'Sleep no more!
Macbeth does murder sleep', the innocent sleep, **695**
Sleep that knits up the ravell'd sleeve of care,
The death of each day's life, sore labour's bath,
Balm of hurt minds, great nature's second course,
Chief nourisher in life's feast,—

Lady Macbeth. What do you mean?**700**

Macbeth. Still it cried 'Sleep no more!' to all the house:
'Glamis hath murder'd sleep, and **therefore** Cawdor
Shall sleep no more; Macbeth shall sleep no more.'

Lady Macbeth. Who was it that thus cried? Why, worthy thane,
You do unbend your noble strength, to think **705**
So brainsickly of things. Go get some water,
And wash this filthy witness from your hand.
Why did you bring these daggers from the place?
They must lie there: go carry them; and smear
The sleepy grooms with blood.**710**

Macbeth. I'll go no more:
I am afraid to think what I have done;
Look on't again I dare not.

Lady Macbeth. Infirm of purpose!
Give me the daggers: the sleeping and the dead **715**
Are but as pictures: 'tis the eye of childhood
That fears a painted devil. If he do bleed,
I'll gild the faces of the grooms withal;
For it must seem their guilt.

[Exit. Knocking within]

Macbeth. Whence is that knocking?
How is't with me, when every noise appals me?
What hands are here? ha! they pluck out mine eyes.
Will all great Neptune's ocean wash this blood
Clean from my hand? No, this my hand will rather **725**
The multitudinous seas incarnadine,
Making the green one red.

[Re-enter LADY MACBETH]

Lady Macbeth. My hands are of your colour; but I shame
To wear a heart so white. **730**
[Knocking within]

I hear a knocking
At the south entry: retire we to our chamber;
A little water clears us of this deed:
How easy is it, then! Your constancy **735**
Hath left you unattended.
[Knocking within]

Hark! more knocking.
Get on your nightgown, lest occasion call us,
And show us to be watchers. Be not lost **740**
So poorly in your thoughts.

Macbeth. To know my deed, 'twere best not know myself.
[Knocking within]   ·

Wake Duncan with thy knocking! I would thou couldst!

[Exeunt]

Key Question

What does Lady Macbeth feel guilty about?

Grade 6

Shakespeare does not show the killing of Duncan. The obvious reason is that this would be too
shocking, too much of a taboo, especially in a play whose political purpose is to point out the

perils of *regicide* to a court. Especially as some of the nobles would be secret Catholics, sympathetic to a **plot** to kill King James.

But a **dramatic** reason is **Shakespeare**'s fascination with **psychology** and the relationship between Macbeth, his wife, and the **patriarchal society**. Lady Macbeth's **soliloquy** is **therefore** really revealing:

> "I laid their daggers ready;
> He could not miss 'em. Had he not resembled (11 **syllables**)
> My father as he slept, I had done't."

At first sight, this suggests that she is simply too weak to carry out this killing. To a *Jacobean* **audience**, this would be logical, and a cause to celebrate women. They are valued as nurturing and kind. They are also valued as being **subservient** to fathers and husbands. So, her decision not to kill Duncan indicates a natural goodness in women, which is so **powerful** that even Lady Macbeth's evil desires can't overcome it.

Some might argue she knew this all along, and always planned to pull out of the murder, to make Macbeth do it. But, **because** this is a **soliloquy**, we can believe that these are her true, immediate thoughts. She went in with the daggers, ready to kill Duncan, and then found she could not continue.

This **foreshadows** her sleepwalking and guilt once she becomes queen. We can see that she is a stereotypical *Jacobean* woman, without the mental strength to follow through on her ambition.

Grade 7

When she first broached her plan, she told Macbeth, "leave all the rest to me." When he proposed going back on his word, she picked up on his use of "we" in "if we fail?" Her reply indicated a change of plan, as they would both ("we") "perform upon...Duncan", together.

The plan has involved her drugging the guards, which has been so successful, that she has decided to carry out the killing herself. Let's consider some of the implications of this. Firstly, it is an opportunity for her to enter the warrior experience that is so familiar to her husband. Secondly, it indicates that she shares his bloodlust, or at the very least wishes to.

Then there is the surprising detail that Duncan looked like her father. An obvious reason for this is the **foreshadow**ing of her guilt. It suggests that, despite all her desperation to be "filled from the crown to the toe" with "direst cruelty", she is still a woman who cannot behave in the barbaric way a man can. This **interpretation** helps those who want to argue that **Shakespeare** shares his **society**'s **patriarchal view** of women as both **inferior** to men, and as weak victims of their own emotions. It also justifies a **patriarchal view** in that women are **inferior** to men, and can only **manipulate** them through temptation, like the biblical Eve and Lady Macbeth in Act One.

What are the 2 main ideas you want to remember so far?
1._____
_____
2._____

Grade 8

So, in the end, she has to rely on her husband. This is a profound moment of failure in her own mind. It is why her first thought is of failure, when she notes that the daggers were ready by the sleeping king: "He could not miss 'em." She can't understand why Macbeth has not already returned. That he could fail to kill a sleeping man is not logical, unless she believes his "milk of human kindness" has over**power**ed him. Given that this is her **soliloquy**, this is unlikely, as he does not mention it.

Grade 9

But another possibility is that **Shakespeare** is commenting directly on the effects of a **patriarchal society**. Despite Lady Macbeth's overwhelming desire to become queen by killing Duncan, she is prevented from doing so by the rules of the **patriarchal society** she wishes to escape.

Her father is the **symbol** of male control. She starts life as her father's property, **subservient** to his wishes, until she marries, when she becomes her husband's property. What this suggests is that she cannot escape her upbringing. She has, in **psychological** terms, been conditioned to accept her **role** as a **power**less woman, and this conditioning is even stronger than her desperation to escape it. Her upset at this is reflected in the extra **syllable** in the line, disrupting the **pentameter**.

Write 3 sentences. Use as many of these words as you can: BECAUSE, ALTHOUGH, THEREFORE, HOWEVER, FURTHERMORE.

_____

_____

_____

_____

_____

_____

_____

_____

_____

_____

_____

Grade 6

The reason for his delay appears to be a sudden onset of madness, brought on by the sacrilegious murder of a king. Macbeth hears a voice which neither the **audience** nor Lady Macbeth hear:

> "Methought I heard a voice cry 'Sleep no more!
> Macbeth does murder sleep', the innocent sleep,
> **Sleep** that **knits up** the **rav**ell'd **sle**eve of **care**…"

Grade 7

The obvious **interpretation** might be that this is his conscience attacking him for what he has done, so that he will "sleep no more". Later in the play, Lady Macbeth comments on his lack of sleep. But, by the time she is suffering with guilt and sleepwalking, Macbeth is probably sleeping well. This is why they sleep apart, **because** her nightly sleepwalking would disrupt him. He also observes later that he had "almost forgot the taste of fears", which implies his guilt does not last long. He is not lying in bed at night full of fear or guilt.

Grade 8

However, it is also true that his early kingship is destroyed by fear, and he seems to take no pleasure in being king. His fear begins here, conveyed in the rapid **repetition** of "sleep", and then his **trochaic emphasis** of sleep at the beginning of the line. "Sleep" also takes the previous line to eleven **syllables**, and the he loses control of the **iambic stresses**.

Grade 9

We can also see that the **personification** of sleep as a knitter, repairing what has **metaphorically** unravelled during the day, as a **feminine image**. This, perhaps, is the moment in which Macbeth kills the **feminine** part of himself, and also then kills the **feminine** influence of his wife. He stops listening to her advice.

This leads directly to an inversion of the **power** relationship in the marriage. Macbeth is filled with **feminine** fear, refusing to take the daggers back, so Lady Macbeth must do it herself. She belittles him for his fear, showing a breakdown of trust, and also that she is taking on the more **masculine role** of bravery:

> "Give me the daggers: the sleeping and the dead
> Are but as pictures: 'tis the eye of childhood
> That fears a painted devil."

Beyond grade 9

But there is another possibility as to why Macbeth cannot let go of the daggers. They satisfy his bloodlust. He ordered the imaginary dagger to "Come, let me clutch thee" and now we see that he is still clutching the real thing.

The usual **interpretation** is that the moment he has murdered Duncan, he regrets his attack against the natural order, The ***Great Chain of Being*** and God. Certainly we can back this up by his worry that he could not say "Amen", as though he has suddenly found God.

However, his **description** of killing Duncan gives us other possibilities:

> "Will all great Neptune's ocean wash this blood
> Clean from my hand? No, this my hand will rather
> The multitudinous seas incarnadine,
> Making the green one red."

Neptune, of course, is a **pagan** god, who predates **Christianity**. As so often, Macbeth gives us a classical **reference** when he is acting against a **Christian** God. Perhaps he is beginning to reject **Christianity**.

Grade 7

His hand is covered in so much blood in this **metaphor** that it will "incarnadine" every sea. This **symbolises** how unnatural the act of *regicide* is – it is a sin which can never be washed away. **However**, Neptune does not wash away sin – this is a purely **Christian** idea, in the form of baptism.

So, if the idea of washing a way his sin does not work, then Macbeth might be referring to his feelings of guilt at killing the king. Just as Lady Macbeth will focus on the "spot of blood still" **metaphorical**ly on her hand, this "blood" is a **metaphor** for his great guilt.

What are the 3 main ideas you want to remember so far?

1._____

_____

2._____

_____

3._____

_____

Grade 8

Perhaps. But another possibility is that Macbeth is shocked at the truth he has uncovered about himself. Once again, it is not that he is ambitious that appals him, it is that he is addicted to bloodlust. What appals him is that he is so attracted to the act of slaughter, that he will even kill Duncan. Their plan does not depend on a quick death, but on faking the grooms killing Duncan in a drunken frenzy. The grooms need to be covered in blood, so Duncan must be killed with two daggers and multiple stab wounds. This will reveal how powerfully he is addicted to bloodlust when he kills the grooms, entirely against Lady Macbeth's plan.

This **interpretation** shows Macbeth's self-discovery that he is this kind of killer, who enjoys this bloodthirsty way of killing.

Grade 9

In this *scene*, Lady Macbeth repeatedly has to take control of her husband, in a **role** reversal of **power** in the marriage. She criticises him for not being her equal, but for becoming **feminine**, which is why she is so angry when she observes:

> "My hands are of your colour; but I shame
> To wear a heart so white."

One reading is that the "white" of his heart is the white of the "milk o' human kindness". Macbeth has gone against his true, kind "nature" by killing the king. But in the moment of killing

Duncan, his conscience has reminded him of who he really is, prompting guilt, madness, and making him react in the *Jacobean* idea of a female way.

But another **symbolic** use of "white" is surrender, which is particularly relevant to Macbeth the warrior. The logical outcome of a **martial society** is that the most successful military tactician should also be the ruler, the king. In this **view**, Macbeth deserves to be king **because** of his military success. When she accuses him of having a "heart so white", she is accusing him of failing in this warrior **status**, and to remind him that he should deserve it as the better warrior. Instead he is being too cowardly to become king.

She is angry that this will stop Macbeth supporting her in her personal battle against the **patriarchy,** to achieve equal **status** with men. Her anger is that Macbeth will not fight to give her that equality. She can't allow him to give up now, when the murder will be for nothing. Remember, at this point, Malcolm should become king. By killing Duncan, they have not yet managed to "jump the life to come". She won't become queen.

Macbeth now gives up his **status**, and raises hers. Macbeth refuses to act, so she has to. We will also see this after his coronation at his feast, when she again must take control. The **irony** is that Lady Macbeth only wants equal **status** and **power** as her husband, but at the moment he kills Duncan she passes beyond this to a **superior social status**. Shakespeare will convey this with the list of instructions and imperative **verbs** she uses when he sees Banquo's ghost.

Shakespeare ends *scene*s with **rhyming couplet**s, which is a convention playwrights of the time used, to signal a conclusion. But Macbeth ends this *scene* without a **rhyming couplet**, which conveys how unsettled his mind is, and how he has destroyed the **social** order.

> **Macbeth.** To know my deed, 'twere best not know myself.
> *[Knocking within]*
>
> Wake Duncan with thy knocking! I would thou couldst!

The conventional **interpretation**, and one which would certainly please King James, is that Macbeth fully regrets killing Duncan, and immediately wishes he had not done so.

But is **Shakespeare** up to anything else? It is an interesting idea that he would rather "not know" himself. This is not the same as wishing he had not gone against God by killing Duncan. After all, if he believes in hell, then he is fully aware of the consequences of killing Duncan before he commits the murder. But the fact is he never mentions the possibility of hell before killing Duncan.

It would **therefore** be very odd for the thought to suddenly strike him now. Instead, the **psychological** horror he is having to face is to face his own desires and bloodlust, to "know [myself[." All his life he has killed in his **role** as a soldier, following orders, defending a country, or a king. Now, for the very first time, he realises that these have been convenient causes. They have masked his true nature, which is that he loves to kill.

We could argue that this is his first moment of **anagnorisis**, where he discovers an uncomfortable truth about himself. This is a stage that Aristotle, in his **Poetics**, says the **tragic hero** must go through.

Aristotle also specifies that the **hero** should have a **peripeteia**, a "reversal", where the opposite of what was planned or hoped for by the **protagonist** takes place. This is the first of many for Macbeth which will prevent him enjoying being king.

Write 3 sentences. Use the words highlighted in the notes (as these are subject terminology).

_____

_____

_____

_____

_____

_____

_____

_____

Build Long Term Memory!

Draw an image in 30 seconds which will help you remember the main ideas.

Label it with 6 key words.

Act II, *Scene* **3**

The same.

Lennox. Goes the king hence to-day?

Macbeth. He does: he did appoint so.

Lennox. The night has been unruly: where we lay,
Our chimneys were blown down; and, as they say,
Lamentings heard i' the air; strange screams of death, **825**
And prophesying with accents terrible
Of dire combustion and confused events
New hatch'd to the woeful time: the obscure bird
Clamour'd the livelong night: some say, the earth
Was feverous and did shake.**830**

Macbeth. 'Twas a rough night.

Lennox. My young remembrance cannot parallel
A fellow to it.

[Re-enter MACDUFF]

Macduff. O horror, horror, horror! Tongue nor heart **835**
Cannot conceive nor name thee!

Macbeth. *[with Lennox]* What's the matter.

Macduff. Confusion now hath made his masterpiece!
Most sacrilegious murder hath broke ope
The Lord's anointed temple, and stole thence **840**
The life o' the building!

Macbeth. What is 't you say? the life?

Lennox. Mean you his majesty?

Macduff. Approach the chamber, and destroy your sight
With a new Gorgon: do not bid me speak; **845**
See, and then speak yourselves.
[Exeunt MACBETH and LENNOX]

Awake, awake!
Ring the alarum-bell. Murder and treason!
Banquo and Donalbain! Malcolm! awake! **850**
Shake off this downy sleep, death's counterfeit,
And look on death itself! up, up, and see
The great doom's **image**! Malcolm! Banquo!
As from your graves rise up, and walk like sprites,
To countenance this horror! Ring the bell.**855**

[Bell rings]

[Enter LADY MACBETH]

Lady Macbeth. What's the business,
That such a hideous trumpet calls to parley
The sleepers of the house? speak, speak!**860**

Macduff. O gentle lady,
'Tis not for you to hear what I can speak:
The **repetition**, in a woman's ear,
Would murder as it fell.
[Enter BANQUO] **865**

O Banquo, Banquo,
Our royal master 's murder'd!

Lady Macbeth. Woe, alas!
What, in our house?

Banquo. Too cruel any where. **870**
Dear Duff, I prithee, contradict thyself,
And say it is not so.

[Re-enter MACBETH and LENNOX, with ROSS]

Macbeth. Had I but died an hour before this chance,
I had lived a blessed time; for, from this instant, **875**
There 's nothing serious in mortality:
All is but toys: renown and grace is dead;
The wine of life is drawn, and the mere lees
Is left this vault to brag of.

[Enter MALCOLM and DONALBAIN]

Donalbain. What is amiss?

Macbeth. You are, and do not know't:
The spring, the head, the fountain of your blood
Is stopp'd; the very source of it is stopp'd.

Macduff. Your royal father 's murder'd.**885**

Malcolm. O, by whom?

Lennox. Those of his chamber, as it seem'd, had done 't:
Their hands and faces were an badged with blood;
So were their daggers, which unwiped we found
Upon their pillows: **890**
They stared, and were distracted; no man's life
Was to be trusted with them.

Macbeth. O, yet I do repent me of my fury, (11 **syllables** – a lie)
That I did kill them.

Macduff. Wherefore did you so?**895**

Macbeth. Who can be wise, amazed, temperate and furious,
Loyal and neutral, in a moment? No man:
The expedition my violent love
Outrun the pauser, reason. Here lay Duncan,
His silver skin laced with his golden blood; **900**
And his gash'd stabs look'd like a breach in nature
For ruin's wasteful entrance: there, the murderers,
Steep'd in the colours of their trade, their daggers
Unmannerly breech'd with gore: who could refrain,
That had a heart to love, and in that heart **905**
Courage to make 's love known?

Lady Macbeth. Help me hence, ho!

Macduff. Look to the lady.

Malcolm. *[Aside to DONALBAIN]* Why do we hold our tongues,
That most may claim this argument for ours?**910**

Donalbain. *[Aside to MALCOLM]* What should be spoken here,
where our **fate**,
Hid in an auger-hole, may rush, and seize us?
Let 's away;
Our tears are not yet brew'd.**915**

Malcolm. *[Aside to DONALBAIN]* Nor our strong sorrow
Upon the foot of motion.

Banquo. Look to the lady:
[LADY MACBETH is carried out]

And when we have our naked frailties hid, **920**
That suffer in exposure, let us meet,
And question this most bloody piece of work,
To know it further. Fears and scruples shake us:
In the great hand of God I stand; and thence
Against the undivulged pretence I fight **925**
Of treasonous malice.

Macduff. And so do I.

All. So all.

Macbeth. Let's briefly put on manly readiness,
And meet i' the hall together.**930**

All. Well contented.

[Exeunt all but Malcolm and Donalbain.]

Malcolm. What will you do? Let's not consort with them:
To show an unfelt sorrow is an office
Which the false man does easy. I'll to England.**935**

Donalbain. To Ireland, I; our separated fortune
Shall keep us both the safer: where we are,
There's daggers in men's smiles: the near in blood,
The nearer bloody.

Malcolm. This murderous shaft that's shot **940**
Hath not yet lighted, and our safest way
Is to avoid the aim. **Therefore**, to horse;
And let us not be dainty of leave-taking,
But shift away: there's warrant in that theft
Which steals itself, when there's no mercy left.**945**

[Exeunt]

Key Question

How many characters are playing a part, while being secretly delighted at Duncan's death?

Grade 6

Macbeth appears to have recovered from the night before, and plays his surprise at Duncan's death convincingly. **However**, this unravels when he deviates from Lady Macbeth's plan, and kills the grooms. This prompts everyone to become suspicious, so Macduff asks why, "wherefore did you so?"

To prevent the guests questioning Macbeth further and exposing him as Duncan's real assassin, Lady Macbeth is forced to improvise, pretending to faint. This distraction is successful, so that many of them "look to the lady". This buys time for Banquo to suggest that they all meet "in manly readiness" later to discuss an appropriate reaction. The fortunate consequence of this is that Malcolm realises a relative, "near in blood" is most likely to have been the assassin. In other words, he suspects Macbeth and decides he and Donalbain should escape.

Grade 7

It's worth pausing to consider the **role** of "**fate**". Against the odds, Macbeth is now the logical choice to be king **because** Malcolm and Donalbain now seem to prove they had their father to be assassinated. This is far beyond any plan Lady Macbeth had, and a fantastic stroke of luck, or fate. So, at this point there might be no tragedy. Just like the **historical** Macbeth, he could have become king and remained so. Again, this suggests his **hamartia** is not ambition.

Grade 8

This *scene* follows close on the porter, who is traditionally seen as the **comic** turn in the play. This light relief offers a **counterpoint** to the *regicide*. Comedy after horror is a **traditional structure** in a Shakespearian **tragedy**, so that the horror is not overwhelming.

However, this **comic** mood continues now in Macbeth himself. Just a few hours ago, Macbeth felt despair at seeing his hands bloody with Duncan's blood. Now, **however**, he is in a completely different mood, as though he has come to accept his own bloodlust and indeed revel in it. So when Lennox recounts a long list of ways in which nature seems to have been unbalanced during the stormy night, **Shakespeare** finishes Lennox's list with an earth quake:

> Lennox: "some say, the earth / Was feverous and did shake.
>
> **Macbeth.** 'Twas a rough night."

Macbeth's short delivery is **comedic understatement**, perfectly timed, like a **punch line**. It also includes the **dramatic irony**, for his own amusement, making light of his brutal *regicide*. This makes him appear quite at ease with his killing of Duncan.

What are the 3 main ideas you want to remember so far?
1._____
_____
2._____
_____
3._____

Grade 9

Shakespeare has given us this dark sense of **humour** before, when the sergeant described how Macbeth "shook hands" with Macdonwald after slicing him open, and then bidding him "farewell". It is a **powerful** reminder that a **society** that glorifies warrior **culture** is **therefore** vulnerable when the warrior returns to society. Warriors are far more likely to continue their killing once war is suddenly won, making regicide very common in Scottish history.

Shakespeare uses Macduff's reaction to finding Duncan to add to this **comic** mood. Macduff bursts into **metaphor**:

> "Most sacrilegious murder hath broke ope
> The Lord's anointed temple, and stole thence **840**
> The life o' the building!"

In this, murder is **personified**. The king is likened to a temple, and then the temple is **personified** as having a life itself. This is a very confusing set of **image**s. Macbeth's reaction is actually to ask what Macduff means, as though to ridicule him, and even Lennox asks if he is talking about the king, "Mean you his majesty?" This can simply be seen as shock. **However**, Macduff's words are quite funny, **because** he is mixing **metaphor**s to such an extent that his meaning is totally unclear.

Beyond Grade 9

There's a brilliant short story by James Thurber which treats Macbeth as a **murder mystery**, a **whodunnit** in the style of Agatha Christie. He makes the point that these **image**s sound like a prepared speech, and not the natural emotion of a man discovering a murderer, **because** they sound artificial. It's almost as though he has planned them beforehand, as though delivering a speech. Perhaps this is his bid to sound statesmanlike, and make a bid as the candidate to replace Duncan.

For a moment Macduff becomes the chief suspect in the murder! The takeaway from this is that Macduff's **language** is overblown and **hyperbolic** (which means overexaggerated) as though he has been hoping this murder would one day take place, and his mind has already prepared a script for it. The effect is to make us question Macduff's grief. His **language** is so **poetic** that it appears almost pre-prepared and insincere. The *regicide* has not made him speechless with horror, but instead given him the gift of **poetry. Although** his words claim that he is horrified, the **poetic** way he describes that horror suggests a secret delight.

There are good reasons for Macduff to have hopes of being made king, or at least a very trusted advisor to Malcolm, when he becomes king. The important job of waking Duncan, when the king is most vulnerable, is not given to Macbeth, but Macduff, suggesting Duncan trusts him more.

The traditional view of Macduff is that his **poetic description** expresses horror at the blasphemous *regicide*. **Shakespeare** gives him this **religious imagery** to make clear, for the benefit of King James and any would be plotters at court, that *regicide* is a crime against God, and punishable by eternal damnation.

What are the 3 main ideas you want to remember so far?
1._____ _____ 2._____ _____ 3._____ _____ _____

Grade 8

This links Macduff to Lady Macbeth and Macbeth, who are definitely playing a **role**. Interestingly, Lady Macbeth has not prepared a script. When she hears the news, she asks:

> "**Lady Macbeth.** Woe, alas!
> What, in our house?
>
> **Banquo.** Too cruel any where."

We can see that she sounds concerned, **because** she begins with the **trochaic stress** on "what", and this places the next **emphasis** on "our". This also sounds wrong to all present – her main worry is not that the king is dead, but that he has been killed in her house. We know she **emphasises** this **because** she wants the **audience** of thanes to feel that she would never contemplate killing him.

Grade 9

But the effect is to make Banquo uneasy – he points out that she should be feeling pity at the murder which is "Too cruel any where." **Shakespeare** also **emphasises** Banquo's distrust by making him finish Lady Macbeth's line short, at only nine **syllables**.

Beyond Grade 9

Shakespeare's educated **audience** at court would also pick up this **reference** to **Greek tragedy**. *Xenia* was considered a sacred custom, and meant that a host had to provide food and gifts for a guest, even a stranger. This was also a religious duty. Not to offer hospitality would lead to a punishment from the gods. Probably the best known story of **Greek tragedy**, the Trojan War, occurred **because** of the violation of *Xenia*.

On the one hand this points out that the Macbeths will also be punished for killing Duncan while he was their guest, "in our house." But it also suggests Macbeth's preference for **pagan** belief rather than the **Christian** world **view**. His punishment is **therefore** in life, rather than to his soul in the afterlife.

Summarise this in one brilliant sentence.
_____
_____
_____
_____
_____
_____

Grade 8

You will notice that Macbeth and Lady Macbeth keep separating in this *scene*. This is a visual way of showing that this is the turning point in their marriage, where he distances himself from his wife. He returns from killing the grooms, but astonishingly at first doesn't even mention it. When they are going to be questioned, he says;

> "**Macbeth.** O, yet I do repent me of my fury, (11 **syllables** – a lie)
> That I did kill them.
>
> **Macduff.** Wherefore did you so?"

Let's consider why he did this. Lady Macbeth's plan depended on the grooms appearing guilty, awaking from obvious drunkenness, unable to remember the night before, and being found covered in Duncan's blood, their daggers at their side. Who stands to gain from paying them for this murder? Malcolm. In front of everyone, he has just recently (perhaps only yesterday) been told that he is Duncan's heir. In this way the murder is perfectly timed, and Malcolm is the perfect suspect. Killing the grooms makes Macbeth the more logical suspect. It's an illogical act.

What are the 3 main ideas you want to remember so far?

1._____

_____

2._____

_____

3._____

Grade 9

So, one way of looking at Macbeth's murder of the grooms is that it is an attack on Lady Macbeth's plan. Macbeth is trying to gain back the **power** he has given up in his relationship with his wife. He has, in his own mind, shown himself to be weak after the *regicide*, and she has emasculated him again, calling him a coward, with a "heart so white." Now he wants to reclaim his **status**, showing his wife that he is in charge.

Another way of looking at the murder is as an escalation in Macbeth's bloodlust. He has enjoyed the bloody slaughter of Duncan, and now, addicted to the blood, slaughters the grooms.

Beyond Grade 9

Another piece of evidence which suggests this addiction is his curious use of the past tense. He has only just killed them. So logically he should say, 'that I have killed them', which also keeps the **iambic pentameter**.

Instead, **because** his regret is a lie, his first line is 11 **syllables** long. But phrasing it as "did kill them" makes the murder sound as though it happened in the distant past. This suggests that his mind is already moving forward to the next murder. It is his bloodlust which cannot be satisfied. This also gives us another **interpretation** to "Macbeth doth murder sleep...Macbeth shall sleep no more." It isn't just that he won't sleep. It is that he won't rest, but be relentless. He won't rest in his pursuit of blood. He will lie awake at night, not troubled by terrible guilt, but by plans and visions of future killing.

Whichever **interpretation** we take, it is clear that killing the grooms now makes it seem as though Macbeth wanted to prevent them confessing who had paid them to kill Duncan. This makes him seem the chief suspect. Macduff's question makes that clear, "Wherefore did you so?"

But we should also notice Banquo's silence here. He is clearly a close friend of Macduff's, calling him "Duff", where he only ever refers to Macbeth as "my lord". Even before Macbeth becomes king, Banquo always addresses him as the **formal** "you". His **language** signals that he is happy for Macbeth to be king. So does his silence.

He knows Macbeth has the **motive** for killing Duncan, and he also knows Macbeth was still awake and wandering the castle as everyone else was in bed. So, why doesn't he expose Macbeth and the weird sisters' prophecies? It would make sense. The first prophesy has come true, and now Duncan is murdered in Macbeth's home.

The obvious answer is that Banquo's plan for Fleance to become king can *only* happen if Macbeth becomes king first. So, he either reasons that Macbeth will become king anyway, **because** that's the way *prophecy* works – it is simply **fate**. Or he believes he has to act, to make that *prophecy* come true. He acts by withholding evidence, and allowing Macbeth to become king.

Later in the play, once Macbeth is king, we will see that Banquo does act – he doesn't believe that **fate** is out of their hands. If he did believe that **fate** can't be altered, he would have no problem telling Macbeth where he and Fleance were riding. Indeed, he wouldn't have to stay away from the castle at all **because**, no matter what Macbeth tries, **fate** would say that Fleance will become king.

Now we know this, we know that Banquo deliberately stays quiet in order to protect Macbeth, and to bring about the weird sisters' *prophecy* about Fleance.

Summarise this in one brilliant sentence.

_____

_____

_____

_____

_____

Even though Banquo refuses to implicate Macbeth, everyone still suspects him, so Lady Macbeth improvises a new plan by pretending to faint:

> **Lady Macbeth. Help me** hence, **ho**!

> **Macduff. Look** to the **lady**.

We can see that she is having to think on her feet, **because** she breaks the **iambic pentameter**, **stress**ing "help me" and "ho", or "help…hence, ho", depending on how we read it. Either way of reading it gives us three **stress ed syllables** out of the four. It is a convincing performance which must distract everyone present, **because Shakespeare** stages a conversation between Malcolm and Donalbain centre stage. They speak unnoticed, as everyone focuses on Lady Macbeth. We also get a sense of how effective it is from the **dramatic alliteration** with "h". Macduff unconsciously takes up this pattern with his **alliteration** of "l". He mimics her speech patterns. Like her, he also loses control, beginning with a **stress** on "look", followed by two un**stressed syllables**.

It might also be significant that it is Macduff who orders "look to the lady". Firstly it suggests that her plan has worked. Secondly, it suggests that Macbeth has ignored her, **because** if he had gone to help her, there would be no need for Macduff to intervene. This is further evidence that the marriage is breaking down, and that Macbeth has partly killed the grooms in order to regain his sense of **power** in the marriage.

The plan eventually works **because** Malcolm and Donalbain decide to flee. They believe they may be the next victims if they remain: "There's daggers in men's smiles: the near in blood, / The nearer bloody."

Malcolm's **metaphor** doesn't just suspect Macbeth, as he focuses on "men's smiles". They suspect that many are happy to see Duncan dead, which gives further weight to our suspicion that Macduff and Banquo are both secretly pleased at Duncan's death.

Secondly, his **image** of "blood" is a wonderful play on words which shows they know Macbeth is the assassin. He is the man "near in blood", meaning bloodline, relative. But he is also literally "near in blood" as he has just killed the grooms.

This also gives us a moment to return to Macbeth's murders. He has stood on stage for a time, unnoticed, before he confesses to having killed the grooms. This strongly suggests that he is not covered in their blood. These have been quick kills, professional, like the soldier he is. This could be why his bloodlust is not fully satisfied. It would explain why he speaks with that odd past tense, as though the murder took place a long time ago. It means it has not satisfied his bloodlust, and he needs to kill again.

Build Long Term Memory!

Write 5 sentences. Use as many of these words as you can: BECAUSE, ALTHOUGH, THEREFORE, HOWEVER, FURTHERMORE.

_____

_____

_____

_____

_____

_____

_____

_____

_____

_____

_____

_____

_____

_____

_____

Draw an image in 30 seconds which will help you remember the main ideas.

Label it with 6 key words.

Write 3 sentences. Use the words highlighted in the notes (as these are subject terminology).

_____
_____
_____
_____
_____
_____
_____
_____
_____
_____

Revise Act 2

Use the next page to summarise what you have learned during Act 2. You might:

1. Draw a mind map, using the pictures you have already used in your notes.
2. Present your learning in columns, focusing on 5 key quotations.
3. Something you prefer.

Quote	Terminology	Beautiful sentence	Context	Shakespeare's purpose	Alternative interpretation	Link to other part of the play

Act III, *Scene* **2**

The palace.

[Enter LADY MACBETH and a Servant]

Lady Macbeth. Is Banquo gone from court?

Servant. Ay, madam, but returns again to-night.

Lady Macbeth. Say to the king, I would attend his leisure **1170**
For a few words.

Servant. Madam, I will.

[Exit]

Lady Macbeth. Nought's had, all's spent,
Where our desire is got without content: **1175**
'Tis safer to be that which we destroy
Than by destruction dwell in doubtful joy.
[Enter MACBETH]

How now, my lord! why do you keep alone,
Of sorriest fancies your companions making, **1180**
Using those thoughts which should indeed have died
With them they think on? Things without all remedy
Should be without regard: what's done is done.

Macbeth. We have scotch'd the snake, not kill'd it:
She'll close and be herself, whilst our poor malice **1185**
Remains in danger of her former tooth.
But let the frame of things disjoint, both the
worlds suffer,
Ere we will eat our meal in fear and sleep
In the affliction of these terrible dreams **1190**
That shake us nightly: better be with the dead,
Whom we, to gain our peace, have sent to peace,
Than on the torture of the mind to lie
In restless ecstasy. Duncan is in his grave;
After life's fitful fever he sleeps well; **1195**
Treason has done his worst: nor steel, nor poison,
Malice domestic, foreign levy, nothing,
Can touch him further.

Lady Macbeth. Come on;
Gentle my lord, sleek o'er your rugged looks; **1200**
Be bright and jovial among your guests to-night.

Macbeth. So shall I, love; and so, I pray, be you:
Let your remembrance apply to Banquo;
Present him eminence, both with eye and tongue:
Unsafe the while, that we **1205**
Must lave our honours in these flattering streams,
And make our faces vizards to our hearts,
Disguising what they are.

Lady Macbeth. You must leave this.

Macbeth. O, full of scorpions is my mind, dear wife! **1210**
Thou know'st that Banquo, and his Fleance, lives.

Lady Macbeth. But in them nature's copy's not eterne.

Macbeth. There's comfort yet; they are assailable;
Then be thou jocund: ere the bat hath flown
His cloister'd flight, ere to black Hecate's summons **1215**
The shard-borne beetle with his drowsy hums
Hath rung night's yawning peal, there shall be done
A deed of dreadful note.

Lady Macbeth. What's to be done?

Macbeth. Be innocent of the knowledge, dearest chuck, **1220**
Till thou applaud the deed. Come, seeling night,
Scarf up the tender eye of pitiful day;
And with thy bloody and invisible hand
Cancel and tear to pieces that great bond
Which keeps me pale! Light thickens; and the crow **1225**
Makes wing to the rooky wood:
Good things of day begin to droop and drowse;
While night's black agents to their preys do rouse.
Thou marvell'st at my words: but hold thee still;
Things bad begun make strong themselves by ill. **1230**
So, **pri**thee, **go** with **me**. (if **iambic**)

[Exeunt]

Key Question

How and why does their marriage and partnership disintegrate?

Grade 6

Now that Macbeth has become king, they have grown further apart, and he begins to act without her advice. **Shakespeare** sets up a **dramatic contrast** to our first meeting, where she and Macbeth were apart **because** of war, and she longed for his return. His letter shows how much he also longed to be reunited with her and her advice.

But now she has to send for him and ask for time together, as though, once he has become king, he has no time for her. And by the end of this *scene* she is silent, with Macbeth having a much greater proportion of the lines.

> "'Tis safer to be that which we destroy
> Than by destruction dwell in doubtful joy."

The conventional **interpretation** is that she is saying they would be better off dead, like Duncan, rather than live with fear and guilt.

Grade 7

But her lines are very **ambiguous**. What is "that which we destroy"? It can't be Duncan, as she doesn't use the past tense, 'destroyed'. It is unlikely to be a person, as "that" is used instead of 'who'. The clue is perhaps in "doubtful joy". Being thane of Cawdor was a real joy, and has now been destroyed. Being together and in love was a "joy" to the partners "of greatness". And now, as **Shakespeare**'s staging vividly shows us, the partnership is being destroyed. This is why they are visibly apart.

Grade 8

"Destruction" here must also refer to killing Duncan. Their "doubtful joy" means they must expect rebellion from thanes who suspect them of *regicide*. But, on a personal level, she has also destroyed their partnership, turning on Macbeth with "direst cruelty", accusing him of cowardice, or lack of love and torturing him with the **image** and guilt of their dead child.

Her use of "we" also suggests that she knows she is equally to blame for the destruction of her marriage. She is reaching an unexpected conclusion, that the love they shared in marriage was more joyful than becoming queen. This is the moment she rejects her own ambition.

Meanwhile, Macbeth would **interpret** "doubtful joy" to mean that his kingship is not secure, **because** Fleance will one day become king, Lady Macbeth may also mean it differently. She is questioning the quality of joy in their marriage, **because** becoming king has forced Macbeth into a different relationship with his queen, so that she must forever address him as "my lord" and "you", and he no longer wants her advice.

What are the 3 main ideas you want to remember so far?

1._____

_____

2._____

_____

3._____

_____

Grade 9

Her words to Macbeth also suggest that it is not killing Duncan which is troubling her, but their relationship. This is why she tells Macbeth to forget any guilt for killing Duncan: "Things without all remedy / Should be without regard: what's done is done."

The conventional **view** is that she secretly regrets killing Duncan, but believes she can cope with her feelings of guilt. If we read her **soliloquy** as wishing that they had not killed Duncan, and that they did not now live in "doubtful joy", then her words are a disguise for her real feelings. She is saying those words to herself as much as to Macbeth, to stop her own feelings of guilt, **because** they are both dwelling on their murder of Duncan.

Alternatively, if we take her words as honest, she is asking him to enjoy being king, and to enjoy their relationship once more. She suggests his guilt is preventing him feeling joy in his kingship. It is also, perhaps, his guilt which is leading him to greater bloodlust. She could be asking for an end to the killing, "what's done is done". She doesn't want his "remedy" to be to kill more people.

Shakespeare makes Macbeth respond to her in animal **imagery**. She has already identified herself with "the raven", with darkness and **symbol**s of death. Now the animal **imagery** suggests savagery:

> **Macbeth.** We have scotch'd the snake, not kill'd it:
> She'll close and be herself, whilst our poor malice **1185**
> Remains in danger of her former tooth.

In this **metaphor**, Macbeth sees himself as hunted by a "snake". The *regicide* is simply scorching the snake, and the "former tooth" who will "close" on him is Malcolm. It is normal to understand this *scene*, beginning as it does with questions about "Banquo" and ending with Macbeth refusing to reveal his plans about killing Banquo, as being entirely about Macbeth's obsession with losing his kingship to Fleance.

Beyond grade 9

But this **metaphor** occurs before that. It is difficult to **interpret** it as being about Banquo, **because** Banquo has not been attacked in any way. It has to refer to their one attack, killing Duncan. This means we can be fairly certain that even as early as becoming king he knows his ultimate fear is not Fleance, but Malcolm. This also makes logical sense – Malcolm is a grown man with resources and allies, while Fleance is still a young boy.

The other reason for the **metaphor** is the way it picks up on Lady Macbeth's **image** of the "serpent" she wanted her husband to be. It is a simple way to link Macbeth's actions with satanic evil, and remind **Shakespeare**'s **audience** that his soul will go to hell for the terrible crime of *regicide*.

The **metaphor** also implies his bloodlust. For example, his killing of Duncan, rather than being the worst sin and murder a man can commit, is reduced to a simple injury, a "scorch".. He describes his evil act as "poor malice". It shows that he is thinking of making his "malice" much worse, so it is no longer just "poor". It suggests he is also planning a killing spree, which will make killing Duncan seem insignificant, and **therefore** "poor".

One **psychological** reason for this could be an attempt to deal with his guilt. If he continues killing, he can dismiss killing Duncan as just one murder amongst many. This fits with **Shakespeare**'s **theme** that *regicide* is such a horrific crime against The ***Great Chain of Being*** and

God. No matter how many people Macbeth kills, it will never be equal to the sin of *regicide*. **Shakespeare** implies he will never be able to dismiss it, and will never get over this guilt.

This guilt is also suggested by Macbeth expressing his envy for Duncan, "Duncan is in his grave; / After life's fitful fever he sleeps well". This suggests he sees his own life as a "fitful fever", and an illness. The "fever" here could be his ambition, but it could also be desire itself. He suggests that Duncan lived the same "fitful fever" as he does.

Shakespeare also uses these words to remind us of Lady Macbeth's desire that Macbeth should have "the illness" which should "attend" ambition. It implies that Lady Macbeth is responsible for Macbeth's "fitful fever". She has supplied that "illness". We can see from his choice of **metaphor**, the "snake," that he is remembering his wife's advice to be "the serpent". This also implies Macbeth has a **nihilistic viewpoint**. Life is not worth living now that he is king.

A **nihilist** also believes there is no purpose to life, and **therefore** no God. This is hinted at with "he sleeps well". Death is simply an end to life for Macbeth and, increasingly, an end to misery. We are reminded of his words as he prepared to kill Duncan, imagining him going either "to heaven or to hell", as though they were interchangeable ideas – not real places at all.

Later, when Lady Macbeth has died, we will see the full extent of his **nihilism**.

What are the 3 main ideas you want to remember so far?

1._____

_____

2._____

_____

3._____

_____

Grade 7

Shakespeare could be implying that killing a king leads to even worse sins, such as denying that there is a god. **Because** Macbeth has abandoned God, **Shakespeare** could be portraying Macbeth as becoming less than human. This would explain the continued animal **imagery** in the *scene*, as though Macbeth is becoming an animal.

> "O, full of scorpions is my mind, dear wife!
> Thou know'st that Banquo, and his Fleance, lives."

The **metaphor** of his mind being "full of scorpions" can be **interpreted** in a really rich way. The "scorpions" are his murderous thoughts – the fatal sting of the scorpion represents the murder he will commit, and **because** his mind is "full" of these, he is contemplating numerous murders.

Grade 8

But the scorpions are in his mind, which also threaten him. Again, it presents him as hunted. It also suggests that his mind is no longer his own – it has become animal like, but also prey to their sting. The scorpions might not just occupy his mind, filling it with doubts and fears, or filling it with plans and desire for murder, but also destroying his mind from the inside. **Shakespeare therefore** hints at Macbeth's madness.

At the same time, **Shakespeare** gives us a sense that Macbeth would like to be cured of this, and to reject his murderous thoughts. Perhaps he wants some help from Lady Macbeth. He still speaks to her affectionately, addressing her as "Thou" and calling her "dear". We can read this moment as the turning point where he either turns away from Lady Macbeth, or where he begins to think of her welfare.

He tells her, "Be innocent of the knowledge, dearest chuck", trying to protect her from the "knowledge" that he is going to murder Banquo. It is as though he wants to protect her from guilt and unhappiness. This is also echoed in his comment, "be though jocund", recognising that she is unhappy **because** he has deviated from her plans. He wants to protect her from the "scorpions" in his own mind.

Grade 9

The linking of innocence and "knowledge" also links to *Original sin*, and the serpent's temptation to Adam and Eve from The Tree of Knowledge of Good and Evil. This might imply he does not blame Lady Macbeth for her part in persuading him to kill Duncan, and realises that it has damaged her as much as himself. He can see that her "knowledge" of evil has damaged her, and he wants to return her to a more innocent state.

Or we can read the *scene* in the opposite way. He keeps her "innocent" **because** he does not want her to interfere with his plans for murder. His **imagery** is dismissive and belittling. Calling her "chuck" is loving, but makes her seem unimportant. He wants to assert his **power** as a king, and as a male, and doesn't want to hear any more of her insults and emasculation of him during and after Duncan's murder.

I favour the first **interpretation because** of what happens next. Lady Macbeth insults him repeatedly when he sees Banquo's ghost, but he never uses a single harsh word toward her. While his mind appears to be under attack, he is desperate to preserve her peace of mind.

What are the 3 main ideas you want to remember so far?

1._____

_____

2._____

_____

3._____

_____

Beyond grade 9

His final words of the *scene* can also be **interpreted** both ways:

"Good things of day begin to droop and drowse;
While night's black agents to their preys do rouse.
Thou marvell'st at my words: but hold thee still;
Things bad begun make strong themselves by ill. **1230**
So, pri**thee**, go **with** me." (if **trochaic**)

They are a very strong echo of her **soliloquy** before Duncan's murder. It is as though he has absorbed her vision of the world, full of "murdering ministers" and "night's black agents". Her reaction, to marvel at Macbeth's "words" could suggest her love for him. She is amazed to hear her own **imagery** in Macbeth's thoughts as though they share one mind.

Macbeth's instruction "but hold thee still" could suggest that she is suddenly moved by sexual desire for him. Or, it could imply the opposite, that she is trying to break away. Given that he is using her own **imagery**, it is very unlikely that she is walking away from him.

Alternatively, we can argue that ending "So, prithee, go with me" doesn't really fit that positive relationship. He has to ask her to come with him, which suggests "Thou marvell'st at my words" is a response to Lady Macbeth's negative reaction to those words. She is trying to get away, **because** she is horrified at what he is about to do to Banquo.

Or that she has realised the "murdering ministers" were no help to her, they didn't give to her the "direst cruelty" she needed to kill Duncan, and she fears that Macbeth is leading her towards more murder. Or, she is disgusted that he will not let her into his plans, and that his use of "Thou" is simply a mask for his lack of love.

Perhaps **Shakespeare** gives us a strong hint that she is rejecting him. Normally, **Shakespeare's** *scene* would end on a **rhyming couplet**. But he introduces a further six **syllables**, with uncertain **stresses**. "So" might be **stress ed**, indicating that Macbeth is having to wait for her to come with him. This **trochaic meter** would also **emphasise** "with", again indicating that she is choosing to be apart from him, and he wants to change that choice. It also gives us an internal **rhyme**, of "prithee" and "with me", which also suggests that Macbeth wants closer unity, reflected in a closer **rhyme**.

However, it is also possible to read the *scene* entirely opposite, as a sexual seduction. Macbeth is playing at withholding. He tells her to be "still" **because** she shows desire. He toys with the idea of her "innocence" only **because** he is going to satisfy her desire when he tells her Banquo is murdered and she will "applaud the deed".

But he makes her wait in order to increase the pleasure of the surprise. He uses her own **imagery**, making himself "strong" through being "ill" **because** everything he is doing is partly to prove his love for her. Calling her "chuck" is a term of love, echoed by Macduff when he grieves over his wife, the "dam" and his children, the "pretty little chicks", and could represent his deep-felt love for Lady Macbeth, just as Macduff's words show the depths of his love and grief for his wife and children.

In this reading "go with me" can **therefore** be paraphrases as 'go along with me in my plans and let me tell you about them after they are complete', rather than a physical going.

Which **interpretation** do you prefer?

Build Long Term Memory!

Draw an image in 30 seconds which will help you remember the main ideas.

Label it with 6 key words.

Write 3 sentences. Use the words highlighted in the notes (as these are subject terminology).

_____

_____

_____

_____

_____

_____

_____

Write 3 sentences. The first words of each one must be in this order. **BECAUSE**, BUT, SO.

_____

_____

_____

_____

_____

_____

_____

_____

Act III, *Scene* 4

The same. Hall in the palace.

[A banquet prepared. Enter MACBETH, LADY MACBETH,] [p]ROSS, LENNOX, Lords, and Attendants]

First Murderer. My lord, his throat is cut; that I did for him.

Macbeth. Thou art the best o' the cut-throats: yet he's good
That did the like for Fleance: if thou didst it,
Thou art the nonpareil.

First Murderer. Most royal sir, **1295**
Fleance is 'scaped.

Macbeth. Then comes my fit again: I had else been perfect,
Whole as the marble, founded as the rock,
As broad and general as the casing air:
But now I am cabin'd, cribb'd, confined, bound in **1300**
To saucy doubts and fears. But Banquo's safe?

First Murderer. Ay, my good lord: safe in a ditch he bides,
With twenty trenched gashes on his head;
The least a death to nature.

Macbeth. Thanks for that: **1305**
There the grown serpent lies; the worm that's fled
Hath nature that in time will venom breed,
No teeth for the present. Get thee gone: to-morrow
We'll hear, ourselves, again.

[Exit Murderer]

Lady Macbeth. My royal lord,
You do not give the cheer: the feast is sold
That is not often vouch'd, while 'tis a-making,
'Tis given with welcome: to feed were best at home;
From thence the sauce to meat is ceremony; **1315**
Meeting were bare without it.

Macbeth. Sweet remembrancer!
Now, good digestion wait on appetite,
And health on both!

Lennox. May't please your highness sit. **1320**
[The GHOST OF BANQUO enters, and sits in]
MACBETH's place]

Macbeth. Here had we now our country's honour roof'd,
Were the graced person of our Banquo present;
Who may I rather challenge for unkindness **1325**
Than pity for mischance!

Ross. His absence, sir,
Lays blame upon his promise. Please't your highness
To grace us with your royal company.

Macbeth. The table's full.**1330**

Lennox. Here is a place reserved, sir.

Macbeth. Where?

Lennox. Here, my good lord. What is't that moves your highness?

Macbeth. Which of you have done this?

Lords. What, my good lord?**1335**

Macbeth. Thou canst not say I did it: never shake
Thy gory locks at me.

Ross. Gentlemen, rise: his highness is not well.

Lady Macbeth. Sit, worthy friends: my lord is often thus,
And hath been from his youth: pray you, keep seat; **1340**
The fit is momentary; upon a thought
He will again be well: if much you note him,
You shall offend him and extend his passion:
Feed, and regard him not. Are you a man?

Macbeth. Ay, and a bold one, that dare look on that **1345**
Which might appal the devil.

Lady Macbeth. O proper stuff!
This is the very painting of your fear:
This is the air-drawn dagger which, you said,
Led you to Duncan. O, these flaws and starts, **1350**
Impostors to true fear, would well become
A woman's story at a winter's fire,
Authorized by her grandam. Shame itself!
Why do you make such faces? When all's done,
You look but on a stool.**1355**

Macbeth. Prithee, see there! behold! look! lo!
how say you?
Why, what care I? If thou canst nod, speak too.
If charnel-houses and our graves must send

Those that we bury back, our monuments **1360**
Shall be the maws of kites.

[GHOST OF BANQUO vanishes]

Lady Macbeth. What, quite unmann'd in folly?

Macbeth. If I stand here, I saw him.

Lady Macbeth. Fie, for shame!**1365**

Macbeth. Blood hath been shed ere now, i' the olden time,
Ere human statute purged the gentle weal;
Ay, and since too, murders have been perform'd
Too terrible for the ear: the times have been,
That, when the brains were out, the man would die, **1370**
And there an end; but now they rise again,
With twenty mortal murders on their crowns,
And push us from our stools: this is more strange
Than such a murder is.

Lady Macbeth. My worthy lord, **1375**
Your noble friends do lack you.

Macbeth. I do forget.
Do not muse at me, my most worthy friends,
I have a strange infirmity, which is nothing
To those that know me. Come, love and health to all; **1380**
Then I'll sit down. Give me some wine; fill full.
I drink to the general joy o' the whole table,
And to our dear friend Banquo, whom we miss;
Would he were here! to all, and him, we thirst,
And all to all.**1385**

Lords. Our duties, and the pledge.

[Re-enter GHOST OF BANQUO]

Macbeth. Avaunt! and quit my sight! let the earth hide thee!
Thy bones are marrowless, thy blood is cold;
Thou hast no speculation in those eyes **1390**
Which thou dost glare with!

Lady Macbeth. Think of this, good peers,
But as a thing of custom: 'tis no other;
Only it spoils the pleasure of the time.

Macbeth. What man dare, I dare: **1395**
Approach thou like the rugged Russian bear,
The arm'd rhinoceros, or the Hyrcan tiger;
Take any shape but that, and my firm nerves

Shall never tremble: or be alive again,
And dare me to the desert with thy sword; **1400**
If trembling I inhabit then, protest me
The baby of a girl. Hence, horrible shadow!
Unreal mockery, hence!
[GHOST OF BANQUO vanishes]

Why, so: being gone, **1405**
I am a man again. Pray you, sit still.

Lady Macbeth. You have displaced the mirth, broke the good meeting,
With most admired disorder.

Macbeth. Can such things be,
And overcome us like a summer's cloud, **1410**
Without our special wonder? You make me strange
Even to the disposition that I owe,
When now I think you can behold such sights,
And keep the natural ruby of your cheeks,
When mine is blanched with fear.**1415**

Ross. What sights, my lord?

Lady Macbeth. I pray you, speak not; he grows worse and worse;
Question enrages him. At once, good night:
Stand not upon the order of your going,
But go at once.**1420**

Lennox. Good night; and better health
Attend his majesty!

Lady Macbeth. A kind good night to all!

[Exeunt all but MACBETH and LADY MACBETH]

Macbeth. It will have blood; they say, blood will have blood: **1425**
Stones have been known to move and trees to speak;
Augurs and understood relations have
By magot-pies and choughs and rooks brought forth
The secret'st man of blood. What is the night?

Lady Macbeth. Almost at odds with morning, which is which.**1430**

Macbeth. How say'st thou, that Macduff denies his person
At our great bidding?

Lady Macbeth. Did you send to him, sir?

Macbeth. I hear it by the way; but I will send:
There's not a one of them but in his house **1435**
I keep a servant fee'd. I will to-morrow,

And betimes I will, to the weird sisters:
More shall they speak; for now I am bent to know,
By the worst means, the worst. For mine own good,
All causes shall give way: I am in blood **1440**
Stepp'd in so far that, should I wade no more,
Returning were as tedious as go o'er:
Strange things I have in head, that will to hand;
Which must be acted ere they may be scann'd.

Lady Macbeth. You lack the season of all natures, sleep.**1445**

Macbeth. Come, we'll to sleep. My strange and self-abuse
Is the initiate fear that wants hard use:
We are yet but young in deed.

Key Question

Why does Macbeth see Banquo's ghost, but never Duncan's?

Grade 6

When Macbeth finds out that Fleance is still alive, he feels trapped by **fate**, "cabined" and "confined." His guilt at having Banquo killed is made worse by the fear that it was all for nothing, as Fleance is still alive, and the *prophecy* is still **fate**d to result in Macbeth having no heirs. This further damages his mind, so that his "fit" begins to take over.

The appearance of Banquo's ghost reveals Macbeth's madness and his guilt. **Shakespeare** does this to show how even attacking King James's distant ancestor will lead to personal disaster. This implies that any attack on King James himself would be catastrophic to the assassin, which is a clear warning to his **audience** of nobles.

Grade 7

In **Greek tragedy** the **hero** usually tries to escape their **fate** – the *prophecy* is something they want to avoid. Then the **irony** is that their efforts to escape this **fate** are exactly what causes their **fate** to happen. So Oedipus leaves his parents, **because** he hears the *prophecy* that he will kill his father. **However**, he does not know that he is adopted. His real father, a king, had abandoned him on a hillside to die, **because** he himself heard the *prophecy* that his son would kill him. Oedipus then kills a stranger, who turns out to be this foreign king, his real father. **Fate** is unavoidable. Then he marries the king's wife, not knowing she is his own mother, and all sorts of **tragedy** unfolds as a punishment.

Grade 8

Shakespeare turns **Greek tragedy** on its head. Macbeth is not trying to escape an unpleasant **fate**, he is deliberately killing his way toward that **fate**.

> "But now I am cabin'd, cribb'd, confined, bound in
> To saucy doubts and fears. But Banquo's safe?"

However, Macbeth is punished for seizing his **fate**. The **alliterative** "C"s create a harsh **tone** in "cabin'd, cribb'd, confined" and these all **emphasise** his feeling of being trapped, "bound in".

Cabined meant housed, or lodged. Cribbed meant, not a child's crib, but a crib for animal feed – it meant to be fed. The **imagery therefore** means that he lives in, and is fed by, "fears".

Because Macbeth has always gained titles and **power** through another man's death, he seems to live in permanent fear of losing these titles and **power**s. He is permanently insecure. This also explains why Lady Macbeth spends so much of her time accusing him of cowardice, focusing on his "fear" and "heart so white". She knows he lives in a permanent state of fear which he is trying to escape.

What are the 3 main ideas you want to remember so far?

1._____

_____

2._____

_____

3._____

_____

Grade 9

He is drawn to extreme situations which invite him to overcome his fear. We see this in his bloodthirsty and reckless approach to battle. We see it in the excitement of following "the dagger of the mind". We see it in Lady Macbeth overcoming his resistance with "We fail", simply facing up to fear and acting anyway. So one way of looking at his behaviour is that Macbeth is addicted to "doubts and fears" and wants to face them.

A further level of punishment in his **tragedy** is that he will succeed in overcoming fear. When he watches Malcolm's army advance, and his own thanes "flee" and join the enemy, he becomes nostalgic for this state when he fed on fear. He says "I have almost forgot the taste of fears". He learns to miss that state of fear, which is preferable to him than the state of **nihilism** he ends up with. **Because** if life is pointless, there is no need for fear.

His most interesting fear is of himself killing Banquo. When Banquo's ghost appears, Macbeth's first words are: "Thou canst not say I did it: never shake / Thy gory locks at me."

Macbeth fears Banquo's disapproval **because** it makes him feel guilty. He has hired murderers **because** he cannot **psychologica**lly face that he has killed his friend. This is also very interesting, **because** it suggests that he is far more upset at killing his friend than by killing his king. This gives us a different **perspective**. **Although** Shakespeare shows that *regicide* is a crime against God, and so punishes Macbeth and his wife, Macbeth himself doesn't see the world this way.

Once he has killed Duncan he spends very little time feeling guilty. His real guilt is in having his friend murdered. When he tells Banquo's ghost "never shake/ Thy gory locks" it is Banquo's disapproval he most fears. His first instinct isn't to send the ghost away, but to stop this shaking of his head in criticism of Macbeth.

This also suggests that he knows Banquo could have supported him. After all, Banquo did not tell anyone that Macbeth probably killed Duncan. Macbeth **therefore** did not have to have Banquo killed. Banquo might just have waited until the *prophecy* came about naturally, without any attack by an older Fleance.

Another possible reason for having him killed is his bloodlust. Notice how Macbeth doesn't focus on the ghost's eyes or mouth. These would be the natural focus on a ghost that was accusing him, or showing disapproval. But instead Macbeth is drawn to his "gory locks". It is the sight of blood which attracts him, just as it did on the "dagger". It is the first thing he notices about the murder, "there's blood upon thy face." This constant focus on blood implies that this is not a **supernatural** ghost, it is a vision summoned by Macbeth so he can see the gore and blood for himself. Yes, it still suggests his feelings of guilt. But it also suggests a fulfilment of Macbeth's desire for blood.

Summarise this in one brilliant sentence.

_____

_____

_____

_____

Grade 6

This *scene* also shows us why their marriage seems to fall apart. Lady Macbeth has to explain away her husband's strange behaviour. She of course cannot see any ghost. She instantly comes up with a cover story:

> "**Sit, wor**thy **frie**nds: my **lord** is **of**ten **thus**,
> And hath been from his youth: pray you, keep seat;
> The fit is momentary".

Shakespeare also the **emphasises** her lack of control here when she has a double **stress** on "**Sit, wor**thy". (Two **stresses** together is called a **spondee**).

Shakespeare is playfully cruel here. Her desire to be unsexed has worked. She has become **masculine** and **powerful**. **Although** Macbeth has tried to preserve her **feminine status** as "innocent" and also hides his decision making from her, she is now taking command in public, taking on the **masculine role**.

The conventional **view** is that **Shakespeare** would be appalled at this as she is usurping Macbeth's **power**. In a **patriarchal society**, this is an example of her going against her female nature, and **consequently** the **audience** expects her to be punished.

Grade 7

This **interpretation** sees **Shakespeare** giving Lady Macbeth the **power** she wants, only to make her use it in ways which destroy her happiness. **Shakespeare** doesn't just punish the Macbeths with the end consequence of their crimes against The **Great Chain of Being**, in death. First, he makes sure they live tortured internal lives, and lose control of their minds.

Grade 8

Lady Macbeth has also taken control at the beginning of the *scene*, when Macbeth ignores the noble thanes and instead talks to the commoners, the murderers. She is quick to remind him of his **role**, and he thanks her, "Sweet remembrancer!" So, **although** the **audience** might be critical of her taking control, Macbeth himself is grateful. She is still his "partner of greatness".

But in this *scene* she is going to have to take command while Macbeth appears to lose his reason. The conventional **view** is that she thinks quickly on her feet, improvising that he has a medical condition since "his youth", and that the "fit" it produces is only "momentary".

However, Macbeth himself tells the murderers that he feels his "fit again" when he discovers Fleance has escaped. It is possible that Macbeth has been hallucinating regularly since killing Duncan, which is why he says it is happening "again". This is also why he sees life as a "fitful fever".

Her reaction to him shows that she is getting used to these fits, and is exasperated by them:

> "O pro**per stuff**!
> **This is** the **ve**ry **pain**ting **of** your **fear**:
> **This is** the **air**-drawn **dagger which**, you **said**,
> **Led you** to **Dun**can."

She is not in the least bit shocked, dismissing it instantly with "O proper stuff" as though she is fed up of hearing this kind of thing from him. Like everyone else, she imagines that he is seeing Duncan, "the very painting of your fear". She **personifies** "fear" as a painter, who paints **image**s in Macbeth's mind. Interestingly, her **imagery** firmly rejects any **supernatural** influence. She certainly doesn't believe this is caused by the "weird sisters".

We can also feel her exasperation with the addition of "you said", implying that she does not believe in his visions. They are, as far as she is concerned, simply produced by his own mind, his "heat oppressed brain".

Her annoyance is also that his reaction has been a virtual confession. Everyone present has begun to wonder if the "gory locks" belong to Duncan, **because** no one knows Banquo is dead. The ghost of the king appears to accuse Macbeth, who replies "thou canst not say I did it."

What are the 3 main ideas you want to remember so far?
1._____   _____   2._____   _____   3._____

We can clearly see this annoyance, and hear it, through the **spondees** which begin each line. We might say the **stresses emphasise** her **stress** .

What makes his nobles even more certain is that the invisible apparition is not just at the table, but sitting in Macbeth's chair: that is, he is sitting in the king's chair **because** he, Duncan, would be the natural king, and it is the king's chair Macbeth is talking to when he speaks to Banquo's ghost.

Thou and You

Notice how he commands the ghost of Banquo, so that it obeys him. His need for **power** and **superiority** over Banquo is also shown in his use of "thou" to address him. It also suggests this love and friendship for the friend he has had murdered.

This is a complete change from when we see them speak together, even when they first meet the "weird sisters". They both defer to each other as having **superior status**, and so both address the other as "you". Only now that he is dead does Macbeth use "thou". Even as king, he still asks Banquo if it is "far you ride" and "goes Fleance with you?" Partly this is his "false face" but the sudden change to "thou" also suggests he could not command Banquo in real life, only in death.

Conversely, Lady Macbeth, even when criticising Macbeth for his cowardly fears, still tries to boost his self-esteem and **status**, calling him "you".

Elaborate. How does this remind you of your own life, or the world today?

_____

_____

_____

_____

Shakespeare is also being playful here. Lady Macbeth ridicules her husband for these visions. But it is exactly these visions which will keep coming back to her later in the play, as she imagines the "spot of blood" still present, despite all her efforts to avoid her guilt. **Shakespeare** punishes her with the very flaw she ridicules in her husband.

Shakespeare also toys with his **audience** here, so that we cannot decide whether the ghost is real. In a **society** which believes in the **supernatural power** of witches, ghosts are simply another aspect of the **supernatural** world. But, he never calls them witches, just "the weird sisters". It may be that no voice accused Macbeth of murdering "sleep", just as the "airborne dagger" could be a trick of his own mind.

Consequently, Banquo's ghost leaves when Macbeth tells it to. It arrives again playfully when Macbeth says, "And to our dear friend Banquo, whom we miss; / Would he were here!" to fulfil that wish. **Because** Macbeth appears to be able to command it, **Shakespeare** hints that the ghost is a product of his own mind. Or, it could be a **supernatural** presence, designed to drive him to madness. I find this **interpretation** more difficult, **because** it obeys his commands in a way the "weird sisters" refuse to until he threatens them with a "curse".

Whichever **interpretation** we choose, **Shakespeare** is determined that the **tragic hero** must suffer every kind of mental torture before he has the ultimate punishment of losing all hope, becoming nihilistic, finally having his kingship taken from him.

> **Summarise this in one brilliant sentence.**
>
> _____
>
> _____
>
> _____
>
> _____

Grade 6

The end of the *scene* is completely unexpected. This banquet was to be their great moment, a celebration of his coronation, of their partnership. Instead, it has ended in turmoil, with every thane suspicious that Macbeth has committed *regicide*, and Lady Macbeth's "joy" has been stolen from her. Similarly, her husband is visibly losing control of his mind.

Grade 7

And yet she has nothing but **sympathy** for him once the thanes have left. It is as though she knows, from this moment on, nothing can be done to save them. From this moment, everyone knows they committed *regicide*. She listens to him and consoles him. Macbeth's first words are:

Grade 8

"It will have blood; they say, blood will have blood".

Here he confesses his bloodlust. His addiction is so strong that he **personifies** "blood", as though it is able to act without his control. And it acts to demand more "blood", which **Shakespeare** conveys through the **repetition** and the **iambic stress** on the last word. Instead of the rage and disappointment she expressed when he wanted to back out of killing Duncan, Lady Macbeth replies in short sentences, and urges him to "sleep" and rest. **Although** this is a very loving reaction, perhaps we can also sense a feeling of defeat, and Lady Macbeth no longer believes she is able to control her husband's fears.

When he continues to express his addiction to bloodlust, she does not try to persuade him to stop killing. He suggests that his only solution is to keep murdering:

> "I **am** in **blood**
> **Stepp**'d **in** so **far** that, **should** I **wade** no **more**,
> Re**turn**ing **were** as **ted**ious as **go** o'er."

One **interpretation** of this is that he realises his soul will go to hell after killing Duncan, so killing more people will make no difference to his soul's **fate**. This fear might be **emphasises** by the **trochaic stress** on "Stepp'd".

Grade 9

But actually, he never mentions his soul, nor the terror of damnation in hell. Instead, he likens it to boredom, "tedious", as though he realises his addiction is out of control. He will keep killing in the hope of feeling that same fear and excitement he experienced on the battlefield, but he knows this will not be possible.

His **verb** choice, "wade" also reveals how he has lost any joy in what he is doing. Kingship has become a huge disappointment to him. It is worth remembering this when you think about his level of ambition. If this were his real **motivation**, he would take some time to enjoy it. But instead he immediately uses it as a position from which to kill without risk, and without fear. Now the **trochaic** "Stepp'd" might convey his over excitement at the blood he is going to spill.

Beyond Grade 9

We can also see in their talk together that Macbeth has now accepted his **fate**. He no longer believes he can defy the weird sisters' prophecies, he can only accelerate when they come true. So he tells Lady Macbeth:

> "I will to-morrow,
> And betimes I will, to the weird sisters:
> More shall they speak; for now I am bent to know,
> By the worst means, the worst."

We can see, in the **repetition** of "worst" that he knows his **fate** is coming to an unhappy ending. He also believes contacting the "weird sisters" is the "worst means" of finding out his future. This implies that he would be better off not finding it out, simply living each day freely. Some **readers** might suggest that this **language** choice shows that he knows they are evil. Others will argue that they simply tell the truth, and that "the worst means" are actually his own evil. As the weird sisters will say when he approaches, "something wicked this way comes".

Write 3 sentences. Use the words highlighted in the notes (as these are subject terminology).

_____

_____

_____

_____

_____

_____

_____

A Note About the Weird Sisters

The **etymology** of "weird" shows that it only came to mean 'strange' in the 1800s, probably as a result of so many productions of Macbeth portraying the sisters this way!

In **Shakespeare** day, it came from the Old English word 'wyrd', meaning **fate**, destiny, the **fates**. By **Shakespeare**'s time the Middle English use referred to the three *Norns*, **myth**ical women (just as in **Greek myth**) who controlled the **fates**.

Knowing this, it is very significant that Macbeth does not call them witches. He does not see them as especially evil. The evil seems to be internal to him. To him, their **supernatural power** is to tell him about his **fate**. **They do not bring that fate about**. They are evil in so much as they are attracted to evil.

This is why they will anticipate Macbeth's arrival with "By the pricking of my thumbs, / Something wicked this way comes." That something will be Macbeth. This sensitivity, like pins and needles, is the "pricking" sense which shows they are physically drawn to Macbeth's evil. It implies there is no joy in revealing **fate** to people who simply accept it as knowledge, and let it come about "without [their] stir". Their desire is to reveal **fate** to those who will take evil actions as a result. Perhaps this is why they are initially silent with Banquo, **because** they sense he won't commit evil to bring about his **fate**.

Banquo is the only **character** who specifically links them with evil, asking "can the devil speak true" and waning that "the instruments of darkness" "win us to our harms". So one reading is that **Shakespeare** favours Banquo's **interpretation**. This of course is the **interpretation** which King James would favour and, as Banquo's descendent, **Shakespeare** gives him authority. **Therefore**, this suggests the witches have lured Macbeth into *regicide*.

However, the other reading is that they haven't – the **fates** simply decide on **fate** – they don't engineer Macbeth's path toward it. Macbeth's desire to "know" reveals he also believes they don't decide his **fate**, they just reveal it. He believes his end is determined, no matter what he does, **because** he knows he is a **tragic hero**. He just can't live with the suspense of not knowing when and how he will die.

His determination to find out is revealed in his urgency. He will visit them "tomorrow", and then regularly, "betimes", **because** he knows they won't want to tell him everything.

It is worth pausing to ask how he knows where they will be. When we last met them, they had "vanished into thin air" and "melted" like "bubbles". Some directors take this to mean that Macbeth saw where they went, but lied to Banquo so that only Macbeth would find them again. This certainly fits his **character**. But it also implies that their **supernatural power** is in *prophecy*, rather than being able to transform nature, control the weather or, indeed, Macbeth's mind. If he knows where, they are simply human.

Summarise this in one brilliant sentence.

_____

_____

_____

_____

What are the 2 main ideas you want to remember so far?

1._____

_____

2._____

_____

Draw an image in 30 seconds which will help you remember the main ideas.

Label it with 6 key words.

Write 3 sentences. The first words of each one must be in this order. **BECAUSE**, BUT, SO.

_____

_____

_____

_____

_____

_____

_____

Revise Act 3

Use the next page to summarise what you have learned during Act 3. You might:

1. Draw a mind map, using the pictures you have already used in your notes.
2. Present your learning in columns, focusing on 5 key quotations.
3. Something you prefer.

Quote	Terminology	Beautiful sentence	Context	Shakespeare's purpose	Alternative interpretation	Link to other part of play

Act IV, *Scene* 1

A cavern. In the middle, a boiling cauldron

Second Witch. By the **pric**king **of** my **thumbs,** (trochaic)
Something **wick**ed **this** way **comes. 1595**
Open, locks,
Whoever knocks!

[Enter MACBETH]

Macbeth. How now, you secret, black, and midnight hags!
What is't you do?**1600**

All. A deed without a name.

Macbeth. I conjure you, by that which you profess,
Howe'er you come to know it, answer me.

First Witch. Speak.

Second Witch. Demand.**1615**

Third Witch. We'll answer.

First Witch. Say, if thou'dst rather hear it from our mouths,
Or from our masters?

Macbeth. Call 'em; let me see 'em.

First Witch. Pour in sow's blood, that hath eaten **1620**
Her nine farrow; grease that's sweaten
From the murderer's gibbet throw
Into the flame.

All. Come, high or low;
Thyself and office deftly show!**1625**

[Thunder. First Apparition: an armed Head]

Macbeth. Tell me, thou unknown **power**,—

First Witch. He knows thy thought:
Hear his speech, but say thou nought.

First Apparition. Macbeth! Macbeth! Macbeth! beware Macduff; **1630**
Beware the thane of Fife. Dismiss me. Enough.

[Descends]

Macbeth. Whate'er thou art, for thy good caution, thanks;
Thou hast harp'd my fear aright: but one
word more,—**1635**

First Witch. He will not be commanded: here's another,
More potent than the first.

[Thunder. Second Apparition: A bloody Child]

Second Apparition. Macbeth! Macbeth! Macbeth!

Macbeth. Had I three ears, I'ld hear thee.**1640**

Second Apparition. Be **bloo**dy, **bold**, and **reso**lute; **laugh** to **scorn**
The **power** of **man**, for **none** of **wo**man **born** (**iambic**)
Shall **harm** Mac**beth**.

[Descends]

Macbeth. Then live, Macduff: what need I fear of thee? **1645**
But yet I'll make assurance double sure,
And take a bond of **fate**: thou shalt not live;
That I may tell pale-hearted fear it lies,
And sleep in spite of thunder.
[Thunder. Third Apparition: a Child crowned, with a tree in his hand] **1650**
What is this
That rises like the issue of a king,
And wears upon his baby-brow the round
And top of sovereignty?

All. Listen, but speak not to't.**1655**

Third Apparition. Be lion-mettled, proud; and take no care
Who chafes, who frets, or where conspirers are:
Mac**beth** shall **ne**ver **van**quish'd **be** un**til** (**iambic**)
Great **Birn**am **wood** to **high** Dunsi**nane hill**
Shall **come** a**gainst** him.**1660**

[Descends]

Macbeth. That will never be
Who can impress the forest, bid the tree
Unfix his earth-bound root? Sweet bodements! good!
Rebellion's head, rise never till the wood **1665**
Of Birnam rise, and our high-placed Macbeth
Shall live the lease of nature, pay his breath
To time and mortal custom. Yet my heart
Throbs to know one thing: tell me, if your art
Can tell so much: shall Banquo's issue ever **1670**
Reign in this kingdom?

All. Seek to know no more.

Macbeth. I will be satisfied: deny me this,
And an eternal curse fall on you! Let me know.
Why sinks that cauldron? and what noise is this?**1675**

[Hautboys]

First Witch. Show!

Second Witch. Show!

Third Witch. Show!

All. Show his eyes, and grieve his heart; **1680 (trochaic)**
Come like shadows, so depart!
[A show of Eight Kings, the last with a glass in]
his hand; GHOST OF BANQUO following]

Macbeth. Thou art too like the spirit of Banquo: down!
Thy crown does sear mine eye-balls. And thy hair, **1685**
Thou other gold-bound brow, is like the first.
A third is like the former. Filthy hags!
Why do you show me this? A fourth! Start, eyes!
What, will the line stretch out to the crack of doom?
Another yet! A seventh! I'll see no more: **1690**
And yet the eighth appears, who bears a glass
Which shows me many more; and some I see
That two-fold balls and treble scepters carry:
Horrible sight! Now, I see, 'tis true;
For the blood-bolter'd Banquo smiles upon me, **1695**
And points at them for his.
[Apparitions vanish]

[Enter LENNOX]

Lennox. What's your grace's will?

Macbeth. Saw you the weird sisters?

Lennox. No, my lord.

Macbeth. Came they not by you?**1715**

Lennox. No, indeed, my lord.

Macbeth. Infected be the air whereon they ride;
And damn'd all those that trust them! I did hear
The galloping of horse: who was't came by?

Lennox. 'Tis two or three, my lord, that bring you word **1720**
Macduff is fled to England.

Macbeth. Fled to England!

Lennox. Ay, my good lord.

Macbeth. Time, thou anticipatest my dread exploits:
The flighty purpose never is o'ertook **1725**
Unless the deed go with it; from this moment
The very firstlings of my heart shall be
The firstlings of my hand. And even now,
To crown my thoughts with acts, be it thought and done:
The castle of Macduff I will surprise; **1730**
Seize upon Fife; give to the edge o' the sword
His wife, his babes, and all unfortunate souls
That trace him in his line. No boasting like a fool;
This deed I'll do before this purpose cool.
But no more sights!—Where are these gentlemen? **1735**
Come, bring me where they are.

[Exeunt]

Key Question

What powers do the witches actually have?

Grade 6

The witches still have the **power** to **manipulate** Macbeth, by giving him prophecies which appear to suggest he is still safe as king. **Because** two of their prophecies have come true, Macbeth knows this safety is temporary and at some point he will lose the throne and Fleance will become king.

However, he begins to realise that "the worst" is coming sooner. He returns to find out when he will lose his throne or his life. The visions they present him give him false hope, simply **because** the weird sisters enjoy creating chaos. When Macbeth wanted to "let the frame of things disjoint", it appears the witches have heard him. Their joy appears to be in disguising their prophecies of danger as implausible. **Consequently** Macbeth believes in he will remain king, rather than see the oncoming **tragedy** of his, and Lady Macbeth's, deaths.

> "Be bloody, bold, and resolute; laugh to scorn
> The **power** of man".

These words encourage Macbeth to feel invincible, and prove that he will never die in battle, as long as he trusts in them and not in "The **power** of man".

Grade 7

The weird sisters speak in **trochaic tetrameter**, showing how different they are to the rest of **society**. To a *Jacobean* audience, this might suggest their evil natures,. It reminds us that **Shakespeare** has used **trochaic meter** when Lady Macbeth, Macbeth or Banquo are lying. It **signifies** an attraction to evil.

Or, just as Macbeth and Lady Macbeth's **power** is only temporary, the **trochaic meter** might simply suggest that they are treated as outsiders, without any real **power** to change **fate**. Instead, they simply use their knowledge to attack the most **powerful** in **society**. Perhaps this is their revenge for being excluded by the **patriarchal society**. Perhaps **Shakespeare** is attacking the **patriarchy** and pointing out how it damages women.

Notice how the "masters" speak in **iambic meter**. They do this **because**, in the world of the play, this **symbolises power** and **status**. It also suggests that the masters are not necessarily evil, otherwise they would use **trochaic** meter. They simply tell the truth, and prophesy what will happen.

The second witch's words also suggest that the source of evil is not the witches themselves. They are simply attracted to the evil of **powerful** men, who can act and spread chaos:

> "By the pricking of my thumbs,
> Something wicked this way comes"

They are not "wicked". Instead, it is Macbeth who is wicked. Most scholars **interpret** the "pricking of my thumbs" to refer to the sensation of sensing evil, like pins and needles, rather than the second witch drawing her own blood to summon Macbeth. This is very interesting, **because** it suggests that Macbeth's wickedness is all his own: the witches are not responsible for it all. They are attracted to it **because** they themselves aren't the agents of evil.

What are the 3 main ideas you want to remember so far?

1. _____

_____

2. _____

_____

3. _____

Grade 9

The witches offer Macbeth the chance to hear prophecies from the weird sisters' "masters". **Shakespeare** may do this to point out how **power**less the witches are, **because** they have multiple masters. He could also do it to show how, as women, they are still ruled by men in a **patriarchal society**. This would mean he is linking male control and **power** to the cause of **tragedy**. **Therefore**, the masters do give Macbeth instructions, where the witches cannot.

> "Be bloody, bold, and resolute; laugh to scorn (11 **syllables**)
> The **power** of man, for none of woman born (11 **syllables**)
> Shall harm Macbeth."

They focus straight away on his bloodlust as his real hamartia, and their first instruction is to be "bloody". They also belittle women, as even association with a woman, being of "woman born" is enough to make them inferior to Macbeth.

Beyond Grade 9

Shakespeare takes this a step further in criticising the **patriarchy**. To defeat Macbeth, Macduff sacrifices his wife, in order to gain the strength of his revenge. Malcolm entirely rejects women in order to be a good king, remaining a virgin deliberately "unknown to woman".

The **couplet** is also delivered in eleven **syllable** lines, perhaps indicating that Macbeth is being **manipulate**d. Macbeth is not taken in by this though. His later words prove he knows someone not "of woman born" will kill him, he just can't puzzle out who that is. He waits in battle, searching for the man who will kill him: "What's he / That was not born of woman?"

Here **Shakespeare** conforms to **Greek tragedy**. The actions he takes now, to avoid his **fate**, are the ones which directly lead to his own **fate**d death. **Consequently**, in order to "beware Macduff" he assassinates Macduff's family. This in turn gives Macduff the **motive** to kill Macbeth. He refuses to fight anyone, so that his sword is "unsheathed" until he meets Macbeth. As we shall see later, we can even argue that Macduff purposefully leaves his family behind so that they will be slaughtered and provide him with the **motive** and strength to kill Macbeth.

Grade 9

The next *prophecy* picks out Macbeth's second weakness, his insecurity and need for **status**.

> "Macbeth shall never vanquish'd be until
> Great Birnam wood to high Dunsinane hill
> Shall come against him"

"High" is **emphasise**d, first in the **iambic** foot, and secondly through **alliteration** with "hill". This flatters Macbeth by **emphasising** his "high" **status**. It works, so that he actually repeats it, describing himself as "high-placed Macbeth". Putting this in the **third person** also shows us how important **status** is to him.

The **emphasis** on "until" in this **couplet** also lets Macbeth know that he will be "vanquish'd", **because** "Birnam wood" will come up the hill, he just doesn't know how it can possibly happen. He refuses to believe it though. The **audience** treat this as **dramatic irony**. They know the five act **structure** of a **tragedy**, and know his end is close.

Beyond grade 9

The witches are prepared to leave at this stage, and don't want to tell Macbeth more. This is very curious. If they fully rejoiced in evil, they would continue to torture him with the **image** of a whole string of future kings, stretching from Fleance over 500 years later to King James and beyond. Banquo's "issue" leads to a long, hereditary line of kings.

> "I will be satisfied: deny me this,
> And an eternal curse fall on you!"

Instead, it is Macbeth's "wicked" nature and evil intentions which force the weird sisters to show him this **image**. It suggests they fear his "eternal curse", and this forces them to reveal Fleance's triumph through history. He curses them anyway, once they have shown him the line of kings, which includes King James, and also shows his line continuing after James, with many descendants. This also implies that Macbeth is most **motivated** by his legacy, rather than being king. He wants to change history. We might **interpret** this over ambitious desire to reflect the level of his insecurity. A secure man of course would be happy to become king when **fate** decides, and never resort to murder.

Because this was first performed for King James, **Shakespeare** is trying to reassure his insecurities about losing his throne, either to Catholic plotting, or an assassination by one of the nobles at court. By **dramatising** how Macbeth's insecurity lead to **tragedy** and his own death, **Shakespeare** could be suggesting that James himself should avoid dealing with his insecurity by murdering Catholics.

Grade 7

Macbeth's **soliloquy** to end the *scene* reveals that he wants to react purely on instinct. Perhaps he knows that thinking, will make him despair, **because** he will realise that he must be defeated in battle.

> "from this moment
> The very firstlings of my heart shall be
> The firstlings of my hand."

Finding that Macduff has fled before Macbeth has had time to kill him, Macbeth resolves to act without thought. He will follow his "heart", his emotions. More importantly, he will react to his first emotions, "The very firstlings", before rational thought can persuade him otherwise.

This complete abandonment of rational thought suggests that he knows **fate** will outwit him. His only relief from knowing that he is going to die soon, without an heir, is in relentless action, and of course more bloodlust and killing.

Grade 8

His **repetition** of "firstlings" also gives us a strong clue at his underlying emotion. This word suggests the first born. It comes from the same **semantic field** as Lady Macbeth's "babe", and of her mother's "milk". This hints at the cause of her ambition and his bloodlust: it is their way of coping with grief at the death of their "firstling", their only child.

What are the 3 main ideas you want to remember so far?
1._____
_____
2._____
_____
3._____
_____

Grade 9

Finally, Macbeth decides to slaughter Macduff's entire family, knowing that Macduff himself will not be present.

"give to the edge o' the sword
His wife, his babes, and all unfortunate souls
That trace him in his line".

We can see his fixation on Macduff's "babes", rather than 'children', or 'sons' and 'daughters', as again tapping into the **semantic field** of his grief at the death of his own baby. Next, he marries this to "all…That trace him in his line". Here Macbeth wants revenge on **fate**, and the weird sisters, who have shown him Banquo's "line" stretching to "the crack of doom". It is a deeply childish emotion, called **transference**, where we take our own feelings and give them to others: if Macbeth can have no descendants inheriting his crown, then he will make sure Macduff also suffers in the same way, with no descendants to inherit his thane-hood.

This is also a clue that Macbeth realises the weird sisters' words are misleading in appearing to offer hope. He knows he still has to "beware Macduff", even though he has no idea how Macduff can defeat him.

Beyond grade 9

There is also a suggestion of worship in his words **personifying** "the sword" as a receiver of sacrifice. The lives of Macduff's family are going to be given to the sword's "edge", so that the sword is like a god of slaughter. We can definitely **infer** that Macbeth has started to worship the act of killing. He even gets satisfaction, now, from killing the innocent. **Shakespeare emphasises** this innocence with "babes" and "souls". The witches noticed "something wicked" in Macbeth, and it appears to be his love of slaughter.

Summarise this in one brilliant sentence.

_____

_____

_____

_____

_____

Write 3 sentences. The first words of each one must be in this order. BECAUSE, BUT, SO.

_____

_____

_____

_____

_____

_____

_____

_____

Draw an image in 30 seconds which will help you remember the main ideas.

Label it with 6 key words.

Write 3 sentences. Use the words highlighted in the notes (as these are subject terminology).

_____

_____

_____

_____

_____

_____

_____

_____

_____

_____

Act IV, *Scene* 2

Fife. Macduff's castle

[Enter LADY MACDUFF, her Son, and ROSS]

Lady Macduff. What had he done, to make him fly the land?

Ross. You must have patience, madam.**1740**

Lady Macduff. He had none:
His flight was madness: when our actions do not,
Our fears do make us traitors.

Ross. You know not
Whether it was his wisdom or his fear.**1745**

Lady Macduff. Wisdom! to leave his wife, to leave his babes,
His mansion and his titles in a place
From whence himself does fly? He loves us not;
He wants the natural touch: for the poor wren,
The most diminutive of birds, will fight, **1750**
Her young ones in her nest, against the owl.
All is the fear and nothing is the love;
As little is the wisdom, where the flight
So runs against all reason.

Ross. My dearest coz, **1755**
I pray you, school yourself: but for your husband,
He is noble, wise, judicious, and best knows
The fits o' the season. I dare not speak
much further;
But cruel are the times, when we are traitors **1760**
And do not know ourselves, when we hold rumour
From what we fear, yet know not what we fear,
But float upon a wild and violent sea
Each way and move. I take my leave of you:
Shall not be long but I'll be here again: **1765**
Things at the worst will cease, or else climb upward
To what they were before. My pretty cousin,
Blessing upon you!

Lady Macduff. Father'd he is, and yet he's fatherless.

Ross. I am so much a fool, should I stay longer, **1770**
It would be my disgrace and your discomfort:
I take my leave at once.

[Exit]

Lady Macduff. Sirrah, your father's dead;
And what will you do now? How will you live?**1775**

Son. As birds do, mother.

Lady Macduff. What, with worms and flies?

Son. With what I get, I mean; and so do they.

Lady Macduff. Poor bird! thou'ldst never fear the net nor lime,
The pitfall nor the gin.**1780**

Son. Why should I, mother? Poor birds they are not set for.
My father is not dead, for all your saying.

Lady Macduff. Yes, he is dead; how wilt thou do for a father?

Son. Nay, how will you do for a husband?

Lady Macduff. Why, I can buy me twenty at any market.**1785**

Son. Then you'll buy 'em to sell again.

Lady Macduff. Thou speak'st with all thy wit: and yet, i' faith,
With wit enough for thee.

Son. Was my father a traitor, mother?

Lady Macduff. Ay, that he was.**1790**

Son. What is a traitor?

Lady Macduff. Why, one that swears and lies.

Son. And be all traitors that do so?

Lady Macduff. Every one that does so is a traitor, and must be hanged.

Son. And must they all be hanged that swear and lie?**1795**

Lady Macduff. Every one.

Son. Who must hang them?

Lady Macduff. Why, the honest men.

Son. Then the liars and swearers are fools,
for there are liars and swearers enow to beat **1800**
the honest men and hang up them.

Key Question

How are Macduff and Ross traitors?

Grade 7

Macduff is such a complex **character**, that it is almost impossible to write about him with less than **Grade 7** ideas. Let's hope he comes up!

This *scene* is a masterpiece in **counterpoint**. **Shakespeare** uses the marriage of the Macduff's to make us draw comparisons to the marriage of the Macbeths. Then he asks us to question the **role** of marriage in this **patriarchal society**. And finally he looks at the **society** of his own time and mocks it.

Lady Macduff has no idea why her husband has fled. Macduff has not asked for her advice, nor even bothered to let her know why he is leaving. She turns in anger and desperation to Ross, who also does not tell her why Macduff fled. It feels like a male conspiracy, a **patriarchal society** which treats women as idiots. She, **however**, is certain that "His flight was madness" **because** she knows that it is likely to end in their deaths.

This is a deliberate **contrast** to Lady Macbeth. She is well aware of Macbeth's desire to kill Banquo, and he also tells her of his plans to keep returning to the weird sisters. Later, when we find her sleepwalking, we see the trouble Macbeth takes to "minister" to her "mind", even while he prepares for a war he doesn't believe he can win. It is a sign of how much he loves her.

Macduff, **however**, appears to have no love for his family.

> "He loves us not;
> He wants the natural touch: for the poor wren,
> The most diminutive of birds, will fight, **1750**
> Her young ones in her nest"

Lady Macduff carries on her **metaphor** of her husband's "flight", and now compares him to the behaviour of birds in nature. Her point is that his leaving was not "natural", and that his first loyalty should be to defend his family, as even a bird with low status in the Chain of Being, "the poor wren", will do.

Grade 8

This is deeply **ironic, because** Macduff is going to kill Macbeth and rid Scotland of a tyrant, defending his country, but sacrificing his family. He appears to have no real love for his family – they are simply possessions, to be left behind with everything else in the castle. Her choice of **symbol**, "the poor wren" is also a wild bird, in its natural state. **Shakespeare** will deliberately **contrast** this with Macduff's **metaphor** for his wife as a "poor dam" and his children as "pretty chicks". He sees them as domesticated chickens. He means this affectionately, but **because** it is **contrasted** with the earlier **image**, we read it differently. Rather than showing affection, it shows that they are disposable, and to be killed for a purpose, like farm animals. We are reminded that he sees them simply as possessions.

> **Write 3 sentences. Use as many of these words as you can: BECAUSE, ALTHOUGH, THEREFORE, HOWEVER, FURTHERMORE.**
>
> _____
> _____
> _____
> _____
> _____
> _____
> _____
> _____
> _____
> _____
> _____

Grade 9

Here **Shakespeare** criticises the **patriarchal view** of women as possessions. The logical conclusion is that they too are disposable. We should **contrast** this to **Shakespeare**'s own marriage. **Shakespeare** was a brilliant businessman, beginning as an actor with nothing, and having to leave his family aged 21 to become an actor. This was certainly high risk. But rather than abandoning his family, he used his wealth to provide the best home for them he could. Meanwhile, he only ever lived in lodgings in London, renting rooms in other people's houses, much like a university student today. His fortune was taken to Stratford. In 1597 he bought the second largest house in Stratford for his family. In reality, this meant for his wife, who lived there full time.

This turns the **patriarchal** marriage arrangement on its head. Yes, we can imagine all sorts of freedoms which **Shakespeare** might enjoy in London, away from his family, and it is highly likely that he had affairs. This, **however**, would simply make him a typical Elizabethan male, living in a **patriarchal society** which placed men's interests first. But, financially speaking, nothing was more important to him than his wife and family.

This **context** helps us **infer Shakespeare**'s own disgust at Macduff's behaviour, and his siding with Lady Macduff. Shakespeare **portrays** how even the evil Macbeth treats his wife better than a typical noble at court. The ironic contrast reveals his attack on the patriarchy. It is a hint that there are **social** causes to Lady Macbeth's desire for **power**. And these **social** causes also prompt the witches to try to gain **power** over men.

Beyond Grade 9

Here, Lady Macduff is desperate for help from another male, a cousin, Ross, who gives her no protection, no help. He only tells her that her husband is "wise", warns her that it is not safe for him to stay, and leaves:

> "**Things** at the **worst** will **cease**, or **else** climb **up**ward **(11 syllables, and trochee)**
> To **what** they **were** be**fore**. My **pre**tty **cou**sin, **(11 syllables)**
> **Bless**ing **up**on **you**!" (trochaic)

Again we might sense **Shakespeare**'s disgust at his treatment of her as "pretty cousin", dismissing her with the hint that, **because** she is "pretty", things might turn out well, even if Macduff is killed. This is **contrasted** with his apparently respectful use of "you".

Almost as soon as he has gone, the murderers enter. Can this be a coincidence? I don't think so. **Shakespeare** could have portrayed the same ideas and **themes** by making Lady Macduff have much the same conversation with her son – **Shakespeare** didn't need to introduce Ross at all. In fact, the conversation we do see with her son suggests that she has already had that same conversation with him. That's why she can now criticise his father's "madness", and call Macduff a "traitor" for abandoning them.

So, one purpose of Ross's arrival is to show the inherent **misogyny** in **society**, where women are seen as possessions of men. But an even more important aspect is the murderers' access to the castle which is, after all, a fortress. The surprise and speed of their arrival strongly implies that Ross has helped them gain entry. Notice how he can't control the ten **syllable pentameter**, and how the first and third lines lose their **iambic stress** . Here is a man clearly struggling with the dishonesty of his words.

Just in case we don't pick up on this, **Shakespeare** makes sure it is Ross, rather than Lennox, who will tell Macduff of his family's slaughter. To make those words seem even more deliberate and deceitful, he plays the same **ironic** game with Macduff, telling him that his family "were well at peace when I did leave 'em."

It is **traditional** to **interpret** this as Ross trying to avoid delivering this terrible news to Macduff. But actually, he uses exactly the same **irony** as he did with Lady Macduff "Things at the worst will cease, or else climb upward." Yes, the "worst will cease" when she is dead and her soul will "climb upward", as though to heaven.

And notice the confession in his words, "when I did leave them." This tells us he was present at their deaths, **because** that is the meaning he is giving to "at peace". It suggests that he was one of the assassins.

Summarise this in one brilliant sentence.

_____

_____

_____

_____

How does Shakespeare use this _scene_ to attack the patriarchy?

Grade 8

Lady Macduff condemns the **patriarchal society** by ridiculing the **social structures** which will place her young "egg" of a son in control of his mother:

> **Lady Macduff.** Sirrah, your father's dead;
> And what will you do now? How will you live?**1775**

Son. As birds do, mother.

His mother **emphasises** the idea that his father is now dead by treating her son as the new thane. He, after all, is the heir, and will become his mother's **social superior**. She immediately switches to the **formal** "you".

Grade 9

Her son points out that she will not have to give him this respect as her **superior**, **because** she can get a new husband. Again, this is **ironic**. She can avoid losing **social status** to her son only by marrying another man, and submitting to his authority.

Her reply is revealing. "Why, I can buy me twenty at any market." She points out that men are in fact interchangeable in their lack of worth. Her husband has not been much of a man, so that she could find "twenty" equally inadequate men in a market. Presenting it as a financial transaction, **however**, also reveals the true nature of marriage in *Jacobean* England. As a woman from a noble family she has been sold and traded in exactly the same way, sold into marriage.

She underlines both how disgusting this is, and also how this **inequality** has made men less honourable, less fair, less loving. This is why any man will do – the implication is that they are all equally bad. Remember that she **contrasts** this with nature, the "natural touch", **because** she believes men have been trained to be unnatural. She is not arguing that men are inherently worse than women, but that their **patriarchal society** has trained them to be so.

Beyond Grade 9

Finally, her vision of this utopia, in which women could buy their own husbands is **ambiguous**. Perhaps she means that men would not be worth buying, and she would learn to do without. Or equally that **because** they are not worth buying as a husband she would simply buy them for her amusement or pleasure: she would actually buy twenty. Her son plays with this idea and suggests that she would then improve them, adding value, so that they could be sold again at market for a higher price, "Then you'll buy 'em to sell again."

Shakespeare presents the idea that men could be improved by women, so that they could be more marketable to other women. He imagines a **society** which actually sold husbands for money and suggests it would be better than the existing **society**, which sells wives for money. This idea is presented by the innocent son again, to show that his conclusion is obvious: even an innocent child can understand it.

This presents the idea that men could be improved by women. How much better might **society** be if women sold husbands to other women? What version of **masculinity** would such a **society** create? Not one where a husband, like Macduff, deserts his family. **Shakespeare** poses this as an innocent question, which is why it is delivered by the innocent son. He speaks with the "wit" of the fool.

Of course, we can take a different **view**. We might decide that Lady Macbeth creates exactly the husband she wants. Macbeth is loving and also so protective that he is willing to kill repeatedly. **Shakespeare** might be suggesting that this is the kind of man who would be created, if women were given control of men.

However, I prefer the **counter argument** that Lady Macbeth's lust for **power** is created by the **inequality** of the **patriarchal society** she lives in. **Shakespeare** is pointing out that this very **inequality** has led to her savagery. It is not natural to her at all, which is why she loses her sanity. **Because** this is a military, a **martial society**, violence appears to be the main way that men are able to advance. Given this, she may feel she has to make her husband more violent, to fit her **society**'s **image** of **masculinity**.

Elaborate. How does this remind you of your own life, or the world today?

_____

_____

_____

_____

_____

_____

_____

_____

_____

Draw an image in 30 seconds which will help you remember the main ideas.

Label it with 6 key words.

England. Before the King's palace.

Macduff. I am not trea**chero**us.

Malcolm. But Macbeth is.
A good and virtuous nature may recoil
In an imperial charge. But I shall crave **1865**
your pardon;
That which you are my thoughts cannot transpose:
Angels are bright still, though the brightest fell;
Though all things foul would wear the brows of grace,
Yet grace must still look so.**1870**

Macduff. I have lost my hopes.

Malcolm. Perchance even there where I did find my doubts.
Why in that rawness left you wife and child,
Those precious **motives**, those strong knots of love,
Without leave-taking? I pray you, **1875**
Let not my jealousies be your dishonours,
But mine own safeties. You may be rightly just,
Whatever I shall think.

Macduff. Bleed, bleed, poor country!
Great tyranny! lay thou thy basis sure, **1880**
For goodness dare not cheque thee: wear thou
thy wrongs;
The title is affeer'd! Fare thee well, lord:
I would not be the villain that thou think'st
For the whole space that's in the tyrant's grasp, **1885**
And the rich East to boot.

Malcolm. Be not offended:
I speak not as in absolute fear of you.
I think our country sinks beneath the yoke;
It weeps, it bleeds; and each new day a gash **1890**
Is added to her wounds: I think withal
There would be hands uplifted in my right;
And here from gracious England have I offer
Of goodly thousands: but, for all this,
When I shall tread upon the tyrant's head, **1895**
Or wear it on my sword, yet my poor country
Shall have more vices than it had before,
More suffer and more sundry ways than ever,
By him that shall succeed.

Macduff. What should he be?**1900**

Malcolm. It is myself I mean: in whom I know
All the particulars of vice so grafted
That, when they shall be open'd, black Macbeth
Will seem as pure as snow, and the poor state
Esteem him as a lamb, being compared **1905**
With my confineless harms.

Macduff. Not in the legions
Of horrid hell can come a devil more damn'd
In evils to top Macbeth.

Malcolm. I grant him bloody, **1910**
Luxurious, avaricious, false, deceitful,
Sudden, malicious, smacking of every sin
That has a name: but there's no bottom, none,
In my voluptuousness: your wives, your daughters,
Your matrons and your maids, could not fill up **1915**
The cistern of my lust, and my desire
All continent impediments would o'erbear
That did oppose my will: better Macbeth
Than such an one to reign.

Macduff. Boundless intemperance **1920**
In nature is a tyranny; it hath been
The untimely emptying of the happy throne
And fall of many kings. But fear not yet
To take upon you what is yours: you may
Convey your pleasures in a spacious plenty, **1925**
And yet seem cold, the time you may so hoodwink.
We have willing dames enough: there cannot be
That vulture in you, to devour so many
As will to greatness dedicate themselves,
Finding it so inclined.**1930**

Malcolm. With this there grows
In my most ill-composed affection such
A stanchless avarice that, were I king,
I should cut off the nobles for their lands,
Desire his jewels and this other's house: **1935**
And my more-having would be as a sauce
To make me hunger more; that I should forge
Quarrels unjust against the good and loyal,
Destroying them for wealth.

Macduff. This avarice **1940**
Sticks deeper, grows with more pernicious root
Than summer-seeming lust, and it hath been
The sword of our slain kings: yet do not fear;
Scotland hath foisons to fill up your will.
Of your mere own: all these are portable, **1945**
With other graces weigh'd.

Malcolm. But I have none: the king-becoming graces,
As justice, verity, temperance, stableness,
Bounty, perseverance, mercy, lowliness,
Devotion, patience, courage, fortitude, **1950**
I have no relish of them, but abound
In the division of each several crime,
Acting it many ways. Nay, had I **power**, I should
Pour the sweet milk of concord into hell,
Uproar the universal peace, confound **1955**
All unity on earth.

Macduff. O Scotland, Scotland!

Malcolm. If such a one be fit to govern, speak:
I am as I have spoken.

Macduff. Fit to govern! **1960**
No, not to live. O nation miserable,
With an untitled tyrant bloody-scepter'd,
When shalt thou see thy wholesome days again,
Since that the truest issue of thy throne
By his own interdiction stands accursed, **1965**
And does blaspheme his breed? Thy royal father
Was a most sainted king: the queen that bore thee,
Oftener upon her knees than on her feet,
Died every day she lived. Fare thee well!
These evils thou repeat'st upon thyself **1970**
Have banish'd me from Scotland. O my breast,
Thy hope ends here!

Malcolm. Macduff, this noble passion,
Child of integrity, hath from my soul
Wiped the black scruples, reconciled my thoughts **1975**
To thy good truth and honour. Devilish Macbeth
By many of these trains hath sought to win me
Into his **power**, and modest wisdom plucks me
From over-credulous haste: but God above
Deal between thee and me! for even now **1980**
I put myself to thy direction, and
Unspeak mine own detraction, here abjure
The taints and blames I laid upon myself,
For strangers to my nature. I am yet
Unknown to woman, never was forsworn, **1985**
Scarcely have coveted what was mine own,
At no time broke my faith, would not betray
The devil to his fellow and delight
No less in truth than life: my first false speaking
Was this upon myself: what I am truly, **1990**
Is thine and my poor country's to command:
Whither indeed, before thy here-approach,
Old Siward, with ten thousand warlike men,

Already at a point, was setting forth.
Now we'll together; and the chance of goodness **1995**
Be like our warranted quarrel! Why are you silent?

Macduff. Such welcome and unwelcome things at once
'Tis hard to reconcile.

[Enter a Doctor]

Malcolm. Well; more anon.—Comes the king forth, I pray you?**2000**

Doctor. Ay, sir; there are a crew of wretched souls
That stay his cure: their malady convinces
The great assay of art; but at his touch—
Such sanctity hath heaven given his hand—
They presently amend.**2005**

Malcolm. I thank you, doctor.

[Exit Doctor]

Key Question

Why does Shakespeare interrupt the action of the play to focus on Malcolm's strange deception about what kind of king he will be?

Grade 7

Because we are writing about **structure** and **Shakespeare**'s purpose here, it is impossible to write at **Grade 6.**

The discussion of kingship lists all the ways a king can be damaging to his country, to the nobles, and to its citizens. This *scene* feels as though it is addressed directly to King James. It is highly **didactic, because Shakespeare** doesn't want Macbeth to be dismissed as a **tragic hero** whose story is not **representative** of men and kings in general.

The **portrayal** given by Malcom lists all the ways a man can become a terrible king so that **Shakespeare** can show King James the qualities he should have: "justice, verity, temperance, stableness, / Bounty, perseverance, mercy, lowliness, / Devotion, patience, courage, fortitude". It's a long list, which implies King James might have a lot to learn.

We no longer have King James in the **audience**, so this *scene* is often abridged in production: it does not advance the plot. Malcolm and Macduff could be discussing anything – a few brief lines, **because** the real drama is coming next, when Macduff finds out Macbeth has slaughtered his family.

So, this begs the question as to why **Shakespeare** includes this long and rather lame *scene* in which Malcolm pretends to be evil in order to see if Macduff has a **moral** conscience or is a spy for Macbeth. This feels even more redundant **because** as soon as Malcolm hears about Macduff's family, he will know he isn't Macbeth's spy.

The answer is fascinating, and goes to the heart of the **historical context** of the play. Macbeth, unlike **Shakespeare**'s other plays, was not written to be performed in his theatre. Instead, it was written specifically to be performed at the court of King James. Indeed, the first account of it being performed in the theatre doesn't come until 1611. The Royal **Shakespeare** Company notes that "An eyewitness account by Dr Simon Forman dates the first public performance of Macbeth at the outdoor *Globe Theatre* in April 1611, though it was most likely performed at Court before King James in August or December 1606."

This five year gap strongly suggests the only reason for this part of the *scene* is the impact **Shakespeare** wants to have on King James, and on the nobles watching the play.

Many noble families would not have wanted King James as a king. The Catholic plotters who planned to blow him up, with the House of Lords, were actually discovered **because** one of the plotters tried to save the life of one of the Lords, warning him not to be present, presumably **because** he was Catholic. One way of reading the **plot** of *regicide*, and the terrible **fate** that awaits the killer, both in this life and in hell, is as a simple warning to any nobles who want to assassinate the king. **Shakespeare**'s message is that the victory would be against nature, against The *Great Chain of Being*, and **therefore** against God. It would result in a "fruitless crown" like the one worn by Macbeth, a reign with no joy in it, only despair, and then eternal damnation.

What are the 3 main ideas you want to remember so far?

1._____

_____

2._____

_____

3._____

He also gets Malcolm to describe himself in ways which would make him appear to be a dreadful king. He lists all Macbeth's poor qualities and pretends he has developed the same ones. But then **Shakespeare** has him claim an insatiable lust, which is totally unlike Macbeth:

> "but there's no bottom, none,
> In my voluptuousness: your wives, your daughters,
> Your matrons and your maids, could not fill up
> The cistern of my lust."

A Note on King James' Homosexuality

Although King James had to be married in order to have heirs, his "lust" was well known to be homosexual, and his male favourites were the cause of gossip and political intrigue from the time James was 13. Wikipedia has a full account of this, which is easy to fact check through American newspapers (as American publishing laws demand accurate fact checking, unlike our own newspapers). The Washington Post notes three significant homosexual relationships:

"But James's most famous favourite was Villiers. James met him in his late 40s and several years later promoted him to Duke of Buckingham — an astounding rise for someone of his rank.

Bergeron records the deeply affectionate letters between the two; in a 1623 letter, James refers bluntly to "marriage" and calls Buckingham his "wife:"

So, why does **Shakespeare** give Malcolm this insatiable lust for the daughters and wives of the nobles at court? It is a wonderful piece of propaganda. James would be criticised for his homosexuality. **Shakespeare** turns this on its head, and wants the nobles to realise how lucky they are not to have a king who is **motivated** by heterosexual lust. At least, he implies, James isn't coming for your wives and daughters! This point is driven home again when Malcolm confesses he was just testing Macduff, and that in fact he is a virgin, "unknown to woman", making a **humorous** parallel with King James.

Henry VIII's reign, and his constant pursuit of women as wives and mi**stresses** was hugely damaging to the stability in the country, and this was just a generation ago. It led directly to the split with the Catholic church, the dissolution of the monasteries, the oppression of Catholics, the Spanish invasions during Queen Elizabeth's reign and indirectly to the Gunpowder **plot** itself.

There are, of course, scholars who believe that **Shakespeare** was also bisexual. Of course, we cannot know for sure. **However**, he wrote 126 sonnets to a male "fair youth", and did not publish these himself, circulating them only among friends. As early as 1640 publishers tried to hide any hint of bisexuality. According to Aviva Dautch, writing for the British Library, "In 1640, John Benson edited a new edition in which he changed many of the poems, perhaps to avoid provoking questions about **Shakespeare**'s sexuality." He changed the gender of the "fair youth" from "his" to 'her'. This strongly implies **Shakespeare**'s reasons for not publishing them himself. We cannot know that the poems were autobiographical, but it seems highly likely. Another indication is that at least one appears to be written about Ann Hathaway, his wife.

At any rate, we can clearly see that **Shakespeare** made a huge impression on King James, gaining his patronage so that his acting company became The King's Players. King James also appears to have given **Shakespeare** an amazing birthday present for his 46th birthday. James C. Humes, in **Citizen Shakespeare: a social and political portrait. Lanham: University Press of America, 2003,** notes that in **the King James Bible**, "The 46th word from the top of the 46th Psalm is "Shake" in "The earth doth shake." Then the 46th word from the bottom is "spear" in "God cutteth forth a spear". Other versions have slightly different wordings with "spear" as 47th from the end.

Shakespeare would not have expected any of his plays to survive for hundreds of years, which is why they were only published after his death. But he would imagine that the first translation of the Bible to be made available to everyone in English would have a far reaching afterlife. The 46th Psalm is a wonderful gift, if true. We can continue to see **Shakespeare**'s play did gain favour with King James, **because the King James Bible** was published in 1611, five years after Macbeth was performed.

What are the 3 main ideas you want to remember so far?
1._____
_____
2._____
_____
3._____

<u>Grade 9</u>

However, Shakespeare is being much more subtle in his **depiction** of kingship. Here he is trying to give King James a lesson in kingship. In particular he wants a king who will not be **motivated** by revenge on the Catholics. He wants a king who will not be **motivated** by greed to take land from nobles he could execute.

Consequently, he makes Malcolm pretend to "forge / Quarrels unjust against the good and loyal, / Destroying them for wealth." By presenting this, in front of the whole court, as an abuse of **power** which James could easily employ, he is trying to show how unwise such an action would be. A significant **motive** for Henry VIII in rejecting Catholicism was that it allowed him to abolish the monasteries. This led to much of their immense wealth being seized by the crown. **Shakespeare** effectively warns James not to give in to this greed.

<u>Beyond Grade 9</u>

There is a good deal of speculation that **Shakespeare** was a Catholic himself. His father and his daughter were both found to be 'recusers', **Christian**s who refused to go to communion, usually **because** it wasn't Catholic. The most telling example is **Shakespeare**'s purchase of Blackfriars Gatehouse, which was well known as a refuge for Catholic priests wishing to escape detection. There is much stronger evidence that his father was a Catholic, and his mother's family was very well known as Catholic. **Consequently**, we can **interpret** these words from Malcolm not just as a lesson in kingship, but also a vital effort to preserve the lives of people **Shakespeare** loves.

Rather than encourage division in the country, **Shakespeare** wants King James to heal these wounds and this conflict between Catholic and Protestant. This is one reason he includes the detail of the English king being able to heal "but at his touch". This is a **metaphor** for how King James should heal his own kingdom.

Build Long Term Memory!

Write 3 sentences. The first words of each one must be in this order. BECAUSE, BUT, SO.

Write 3 sentences. Use the words highlighted in the notes (as these are subject terminology).

_____

_____

_____

_____

_____

_____

_____

_____

_____

_____

Draw an image in 30 seconds which will help you remember the main ideas.

Label it with 6 key words.

[Enter ROSS]

Macduff. See, who comes here?

Malcolm. My countryman; but yet I know him not.**2025**

Macduff. My ever-gentle cousin, welcome hither.

Malcolm. I know him now. Good God, betimes remove
The means that makes us strangers!

Ross. Sir, amen.

Macduff. Stands Scotland where it did?**2030**

Ross. Alas, poor country!
Almost afraid to know itself. It cannot
Be call'd our mother, but our grave; where nothing,
But who knows nothing, is once seen to smile;
Where sighs and groans and shrieks that rend the air **2035**
Are made, not mark'd; where violent sorrow seems
A modern ecstasy; the dead man's knell
Is there scarce ask'd for who; and good men's lives
Expire before the flowers in their caps,
Dying or ere they sicken.**2040**

Macduff. O, relation
Too nice, and yet too true!

Malcolm. What's the newest grief?

Ross. That of an hour's age doth hiss the speaker:
Each minute teems a new one.**2045**

Macduff. How does my wife?

Ross. Why, well.

Macduff. And all my children?

Ross. Well too.

Macduff. The tyrant has not batter'd at their peace?**2050**

Ross. No; they were well at peace when I did leave 'em.

Macduff. But not a niggard of your speech: how goes't?

Ross. When I came hither to transport the tidings,
Which I have heavily borne, there ran a rumour
Of many worthy fellows that were out; **2055**
Which was to my belief witness'd the rather,
For that I saw the tyrant's **power** a-foot:
Now is the time of help; your eye in Scotland
Would create soldiers, make our women fight,
To doff their dire di**stresses.2060**

Malcolm. Be't their comfort
We are coming thither: gracious England hath
Lent us good Siward and ten thousand men;
An older and a better soldier none
That Christendom gives out.**2065**

Ross. Would I could answer
This comfort with the like! But I have words
That would be howl'd out in the desert air,
Where hearing should not latch them.

Macduff. What concern they? **2070**
The general cause? or is it a fee-grief
Due to some single breast?

Ross. No mind that's honest
But in it shares some woe; though the main part
Pertains to you alone.**2075**

Macduff. If it be mine,
Keep it not from me, quickly let me have it.

Ross. Let not your ears despise my tongue for ever,
Which shall possess them with the heaviest sound
That ever yet they heard.**2080**

Macduff. Hum! I guess at it.

Ross. Your castle is surprised; your wife and babes
Savagely slaughter'd: to relate the manner, (11 **syllables**)
Were, on the quarry of these murder'd deer,
To add the death of you.**2085**

Malcolm. Merciful heaven!
What, man! ne'er pull your hat upon your brows;
Give sorrow words: the grief that does not speak
Whispers the o'er-fraught heart and bids it break.

Macduff. My children too?**2090**

Ross. Wife, children, servants, all
That could be found.

Macduff. And I must be from thence!
My wife kill'd too?

Ross. I have said.**2095**

Malcolm. Be comforted:
Let's make us medicines of our great revenge,
To cure this deadly grief.

Macduff. He has no children. All my pretty ones?
Did you say all? O hell-kite! All? **2100** (8 **syllables**)
What, all my pretty chickens and their dam
At one fell swoop?

Malcolm. Dispute it like a man.

Macduff. I shall do so;
But I must also feel it as a man: **2105**
I cannot but remember such things were,
That were most precious to me. Did heaven look on, (12 **syllables**)
And would not take their part? Sinful Macduff,
They were all struck for thee! naught that I am,
Not for their own demerits, but for mine, **2110**
Fell slaughter on their souls. Heaven rest them now!

Malcolm. Be this the whetstone of your sword: let grief
Convert to anger; blunt not the heart, enrage it.

Macduff. O, I could play the woman with mine eyes
And braggart with my tongue! But, gentle heavens, **2115**
Cut short all intermission; front to front
Bring thou this fiend of Scotland and myself;
Within my sword's length set him; if he 'scape,
Heaven forgive him too!

Malcolm. This tune goes manly. **2120**
Come, go we to the king; our **power** is ready;
Our lack is nothing but our leave; Macbeth
Is ripe for shaking, and the **power**s above
Put on their instruments. Receive what cheer you may:
The night is long that never finds the day.**2125**

[Exeunt]

Key Question

Why did Macduff leave his wife and children behind?

Grade 7

The first few lines fit this drama perfectly. Malcolm asks, "Why in that rawness left you wife and child, / Those precious **motives**, those strong knots of love"? Malcolm means he cannot trust Macduff, **because** his decision to leave his "precious" family is reckless. He is leaving them to face "rawness" which the **audience** has just seen in the slaughter of Macduff's family. **Shakespeare**, **however**, means more than this. Lady Macduff accused her husband of lacking love, and being "a traitor" for leaving them.

He suggests that Macduff has sacrificed them in order to have the same "spur to prick the sides of [his] intent". Just as Macbeth knew that writing to Lady Macbeth would encourage her to persuade him to commit *regicide*, so Macduff knows that leaving his wife and family behind will lead to his profound desire for revenge. If Macduff were a **hero** of a **tragic** play, then his **hamartia** is the sacrifice of his family, to give him the rage to kill Macbeth.

Grade 8

We can begin to read Macduff as Macbeth's **mirror image** or **alter ego**. He too will lose all his children. He too will have no "line" of heirs to follow him. Both have wives who claim they are not loved enough. He too will lose his wife, who dies before him. He too was Banquo's close friend, so much so that Banquo called him "Duff". **Shakespeare** appears to **construct** him as Macbeth's opposite. Macbeth will enjoy slaughter, but Macduff will refuse to kill, saving his sword only to fight Macbeth. There are strong hints that he loses this battle, and Macbeth is about to kill him, until Macbeth hears the truth of his birth and is then killed by Macduff.

This *scene* tells us so much about Macduff. He has shown himself to be honourable, in that he will not fight for Malcolm when he believes he would be a worse king than Macbeth. **However**, **Shakespeare** makes us question whether any of these warriors is truly honourable. He **contrasts** this with Macduff's honour as a husband. **Shakespeare** makes Macduff ask Ross: "The tyrant has not batter'd at their peace?" We can see immediately that he knows leaving them would lead to an attack by Macbeth, the "tyrant". We might generously **interpret** "batter'd" to imply that he thought their castle would be attacked, buy not overrun. This offers the further possibility, which Roman Polanski showed in his film of the play, that Ross is actually a traitor who has opened the castle to the gang of murderers sent by Macbeth.

Grade 9

Again, **Shakespeare** makes us confront Macduff's decision to abandon his family, and be horrified. In this **context**, his **metaphor** for the death of his children and wife, "all my pretty chickens and their dam" seems both insulting and revealing. They are not even favourite pets, but farmyard animals. There is a terrible hint that he has calculated some would die, through the **repetition** of "all" and is shocked that "all" have been slaughtered. He had expected only some to be killed.

Beyond Grade 9

His grief is certainly genuine. But **Shakespeare** shows that this is simply not enough. He should be feeling guilt and shame. He blames himself only **because** he has angered Macbeth with his "demerits". But he doesn't blame himself for abandoning them deliberately as targets. He even blames God for "looking on". **However**, the addition of "heaven" to this line brings it to twelve **syllables**, revealing that blaming "heaven" is a convenient lie to take away his own responsibility.

Macduff's desire for revenge soon follows. Malcom tells him to use his grief to give him the "anger" he will need to kill Macbeth. **However**, Macduff tells Malcolm "But I must also feel it as a man". A charitable **interpretation** is that Macduff is giving Malcolm a lesson in kingship, or at least in **masculinity**. A real "man" is not simply a man of action, but is able to feel and **empathise** with others.

But I don't accept that. He has engineered the slaughter of his family. Now he wants to feel the full impact of their death. He has created his own "spur" to his ambition to kill Macbeth, and sacrificed his own family in order to give him the necessary strength and rage to fight Macbeth.

Build Long Term Memory!

Go back over this whole section and pick out the top 5 ideas you need to remember.

1._____

_____

2._____

_____

3._____

_____

4._____

_____

5._____

Write 3 sentences. Use the words highlighted in the notes (as these are subject terminology).

_____

_____

_____

_____

_____

_____

_____

_____

_____

Draw an image in 30 seconds which will help you remember the main ideas.

Label it with 6 key words.

Write 3 sentences. The first words of each one must be in this order. **BECAUSE**, BUT, SO.

_____

_____

_____

_____

_____

_____

_____

Revise Act 4

Use the next page to summarise what you have learned during Act 4. You might:

1. Draw a mind map, using the pictures you have already used in your notes.
2. Present your learning in columns, focusing on 5 key quotations.
3. Something you prefer.

Quote	Terminology	Beautiful sentence	Context	Shakespeare's purpose	Alternative interpretation	Link to other part of play

Act V, *Scene* 1

Dunsinane. Ante-room in the castle.

[Enter a Doctor of Physic and a Waiting-Gentlewoman]

Doctor. I have two nights watched with you, but can perceive
no truth in your report. When was it she last walked?

Gentlewoman. Since his majesty went into the field, I have seen **2130**
her rise from her bed, throw her night-gown upon
her, unlock her closet, take forth paper, fold it,
write upon't, read it, afterwards seal it, and again
return to bed; yet all this while in a most fast sleep.

Doctor. A great perturbation in nature, to receive at once **2135**
the benefit of sleep, and do the effects of
watching! In this slumbery agitation, besides her
walking and other actual performances, what, at any
time, have you heard her say?

Gentlewoman. That, sir, which I will not report after her.**2140**

Doctor. You may to me: and 'tis most meet you should.

Gentlewoman. Neither to you nor any one; having no witness to
confirm my speech.
[Enter LADY MACBETH, with a taper]
Lo you, here she comes! This is her very guise; **2145**
and, upon my life, fast asleep. Observe her; stand close.

Doctor. How came she by that light?

Gentlewoman. Why, it stood by her: she has light by her
continually; 'tis her command.

Doctor. You see, her eyes are open.**2150**

Gentlewoman. Ay, but their sense is shut.

Doctor. What is it she does now? Look, how she rubs her hands.

Gentlewoman. It is an accustomed action with her, to seem thus
washing her hands: I have known her continue in
this a quarter of an hour.**2155**

Lady Macbeth. Yet here's a spot.

Doctor. Hark! she speaks: I will set down what comes from
her, to satisfy my remembrance the more strongly.

Lady Macbeth. Out, damned spot! out, I say!—One: two: why, then, 'tis time to do't.—Hell is murky!—Fie, my **2160** lord, fie! a soldier, and afeard? What need we fear who knows it, when none can call our **power** to account?—Yet who would have thought the old man to have had so much blood in him.

Doctor. Do you mark that?**2165**

Lady Macbeth. The thane of Fife had a wife: where is she now?— What, will these hands ne'er be clean?—No more o' that, my lord, no more o' that: you mar all with this starting.

Doctor. Go to, go to; you have known what you should not.**2170**

Gentlewoman. She has spoke what she should not, I am sure of that: heaven knows what she has known.

Lady Macbeth. Here's the smell of the blood still: all the perfumes of Arabia will not sweeten this little hand. Oh, oh, oh!**2175**

Doctor. What a sigh is there! The heart is sorely charged.

Gentlewoman. I would not have such a heart in my bosom for the dignity of the whole body.

Doctor. Well, well, well,—

Gentlewoman. Pray God it be, sir.**2180**

Doctor. This disease is beyond my practise: yet I have known those which have walked in their sleep who have died holily in their beds.

Lady Macbeth. Wash your hands, put on your nightgown; look not so pale.—I tell you yet again, Banquo's buried; he **2185** cannot come out on's grave.

Doctor. Even so?

Lady Macbeth. To bed, to bed! there's knocking at the gate: come, come, come, come, give me your hand. What's done cannot be undone.—To bed, to bed, to bed!**2190**

[Exit]

Doctor. Will she go now to bed?

Gentlewoman. Directly.

Doctor. Foul whisperings are abroad: unnatural deeds
Do breed unnatural troubles: infected minds 2195
To their deaf pillows will discharge their secrets:
More needs she the divine than the physician.
God, God forgive us all! Look after her;

[Exeunt]

Key Question

Why does Lady Macbeth sleepwalk?

Grade 6

Lady Macbeth is deeply affected, not just by her part in killing Duncan, but by everything else which has happened. Her sleepwalking is a symptom and **symbol** of her guilt in persuading Macbeth to kill Duncan, so "the smell of blood still" stays with her. Smell has the most impact on memory and also cannot be easily disguised. This suggests she feels even more guilt **because** everyone knows of her part in the plot, as they can **symbolically** smell it. This is also revealed by "all the perfumes of Arabia" not being enough to hide it.

This further implies that her guilt is so great that God can never forgive it, and helps reinforce **Shakespeare**'s political message that *regicide* leads both to madness and eternal damnation.

Grade 7

We should notice that this most famous of Lady Macbeth's **soliloquys** is also delivered in **prose**, sometimes **iambic**, sometimes **trochaic**, with lines of irregular length. Partly this reflects her troubled mind, unable to organise itself. But **Shakespeare** also uses it to reveal her loss of **status**, so she cannot speak in **iambic pentameter**. This **symbolises** how her soul has lost **status**, and will go to hell, of course.

Grade 8

Yet what other forms of **status** might be lost? As queen, she now sleeps apart from her husband. **Shakespeare** wants us to realise that Macbeth is not present. Apparently the "light" would prevent him sleeping. The **irony** of "Macbeth doth murder sleep" is that it appears he now sleeps well, but his wife does not. Her sleep has been murdered. It seems that Macbeth has accepted his **fate**, while Lady Macbeth fears hers, and so can't sleep. This is another reason to suggest that Macbeth does not really believe in the concept of hell.

She has also lost **status** within nature. Not only is she unnatural, asking to be unsexed and purged of the "milk" which **symbolised** a woman's nurturing nature, she has also damaged her sanity. She hallucinates the "damned spot" while Macbeth is no longer having visions. We can definitely argue that **Shakespeare**'s **audience** will want her to be punished for turning against the **role society** gives her gender. This is why, before her death, **Shakespeare** first drives her mad.

As usual, **Shakespeare** uses **contrast** to reveal the change in his **character** since we first met her. Where she began the play praising the dark **power**s of nature, **symbolised** by "the raven" and of the **supernatural** with "the dunnest smoke of hell", now she is addicted to "light".

Shakespeare makes us pay attention to this by having the doctor ask about her light. The reply, "Why, it stood by her: she has light by her / continually; 'tis her command" shows her desperation to escape her past self: she has light "continually" and does not ever let it go out, which is "her command". This **symbolises** her regret at killing Duncan in the first place. It also reveals her fear of hell, **because** "light" is **symbolic** of God in the **Christian** tradition. We know she means it in this **symbolic** way **because** this light is useless to her: she can't see it **because** she is sleepwalking.

Grade 9

Even the phrase "stood by her" reveals her **symbolic** meaning. She wants God to stand by her, to save her soul from hell. Her sleepwalking must partly be caused by the certain knowledge that this cannot happen.

When she speaks, she is also focused on hell. "Out, damned spot! out, I say!—One: two: why, / then, 'tis time to do't.—Hell is murky!"

She tries to distance herself from her soul's damnation by calling the spot of blood "damned", as though if she could just clean that off, her soul would be saved. This reveals her desperation. It also reinforces **Shakespeare**'s **theme** in dissuading his watching **audience** of nobles from *regicide*.

Her sleepwalking is also caused by, in her dreams, becoming Macbeth. When she says "One: two: why / then tis time to do't", these are Macbeth's thoughts. He is waiting for her to signal with two rings of the bell, thinking "the bell invites me." This suggests that she is also horrified at what she feels she has made Macbeth do, and so actually dreams of herself as Macbeth.

Write 3 sentences. Use the words highlighted in the notes (as these are subject terminology).

_____

_____

_____

_____

_____

_____

_____

Beyond Grade 9

Perhaps she feels that she has created a monster. Her dream leaps from their first crime to Macbeth's latest, "The thane of Fife had a wife: where is she now?" Most importantly, she is troubled by Macbeth's killing of the innocent, Macduff's family. Perhaps she also focuses on his "wife" **because** she is making a comparison to her own **status**. Clearly, Macbeth's "firstlings of the heart" mean that he no longer consults her. She has been marginalised, and can see that her **role** as "wife" is now dead. Similarly, they appear to be no longer sleeping together, and perhaps their sexual relationship is also dead.

The internal **rhyme** of "Fife" and "wife" also gives this line a childlike, nursery **rhyme** quality. This might imply that she is regressing mentally, losing her adult identity, and trying to find a time when she felt more innocent, less "damned".

Another possibility is that she is trying not to think of all Macduff's slaughtered children, **because** it is a painful reminder of her own dead child. Yet she fails in this, and so speaks in verse like a nursery **rhyme**. The final question, "where is she now?" also invites her unspoken answer: heaven. This again is **juxtaposed** with her soul's destination: hell.

Grade 7

Next, **Shakespeare** focuses on the senses. Where Macbeth was tricked by his sense of "sight", she is tricked by "smell": "Here's the smell of the blood still: all the / perfumes of Arabia will not sweeten this little / hand. Oh, oh, oh!"

This "smell" is much more **powerful**. Macbeth can look elsewhere, or even command Banquo's ghost to "quit my sight" and be obeyed. But even when she closes her eyes, Lady Macbeth can't escape "the smell of blood still". This shows how her sense of guilt is much greater than Macbeth's.

Grade 8

The "perfumes of Arabia" are the best that money can buy, **symbolising** how her **status** as queen has been worthless. The joy of being queen has brought is destroyed by the guilt at what she has done. "Arabia" also **symbolises** great distance, and her desire to escape her present state.

Shakespeare uses it as an echo of Macbeth's lament that "all great Neptune's oceans" wouldn't wash the blood from his hands. The way they echo each other's thoughts and **imagery** **symbolises** their partnership, and perhaps their continuing love for each other. This explains why Macbeth has tried to keep her "innocent" of his murderous plans, as though realising the **psychological** damage her guilt is causing her.

This is suggested by how Lady Macbeth also focuses on innocence. She **characterises** her hand as "little" in the hope that it is too small to be so guilty. The desire for it to "sweeten" is also a childlike use of perfume, rather than to be used for sexual attraction as a woman. She is regressing into this childlike state to escape responsibility for what she has done.

Grade 9

We also notice her use of the **triplet** throughout this *scene*. Again it is a childlike feature, used in so many story **structures** for children. But in this play it is also a strong reminder of the three witches. Her "Oh, oh, oh" is a subtle reminder of them. **However**, given that this *scene* explores her most intimate and profound regrets, the witches are not mentioned. Nor does she mention her desire to be unsexed, nor her desire to seek the aid of "murdering ministers".

On one level, this implies that she does not really believe in the **power** of the **supernatural**. This is reinforced by her refusal in this *scene* to believe in the ability of Banquo to return as a ghost. It hints, perhaps, at **Shakespeare**'s own lack of belief in witchcraft. At another level, she is taking full responsibility for what she has done. She certainly does not blame the witches.

Her final words focus on her marriage: "What's / done cannot be undone.—To bed, to bed, to bed!" In the first part she tells herself that her guilt serves no purpose, and she must accept what she has done. The second part, inviting Macbeth "To bed, to bed, to bed", indicates both a sexual passion for her husband, and a plea that he should let her soothe his mind, and relieve his guilt.

> **Write 3 sentences. Use the words highlighted in the notes (as these are subject terminology).**
>
> _____
>
> _____
>
> _____
>
> _____
>
> _____
>
> _____
>
> _____

Beyond Grade 9

She has succeeded in this. Macbeth is no longer troubled by his lack of sleep, nor by his guilt. His reaction to his crime is still to continue killing, **because** he has already accepted that his kingship is a "fruitless crown". He, as we shall see, now has a **nihilistic view** of life and God, perhaps even an atheistic **view**.

Whereas Lady Macbeth is still defined by the **patriarchal society** which has made her. She still believes in God, in heaven and "hell". She still believes in being **feminine**, focusing on "perfume", her "little hand", the **image** of the "wife". She still believes in serving her husband. It is interesting that, even in her dreams, she still addresses Macbeth **formal**ly as "my Lord" and "your" and is still **subservient** to his **status**.

Shakespeare implies that this is the cause of her **tragedy**. Each time she sleepwalks, her speech begins with her guilt. **Shakespeare** makes the doctor ask if she will now go to bed, and the gentlewoman has no hesitation in saying "directly". We did not need to be told this. **Shakespeare** needs us to understand that this is the part of her sleepwalking she cannot escape – she returns to bed with Macbeth in her imagination **because**, in her real bed, she is alone. It is her failure as a wife, or his failure as a husband, which seems to upset her dreams most.

Ultimately, perhaps, she commits suicide **because** their love for each other is poisoned by what they have done. They love at a distance despite living side by side. **Ironic**ally, it is her failure in the **role society** has given her as a "wife" which leads to her despair and suicide, much more than her guilt.

> **Summarise this in one brilliant sentence.**
>
> _____
>
> _____
>
> _____
>
> _____

Write 3 sentences. Use as many of these words as you can: **BECAUSE, ALTHOUGH, THEREFORE, HOWEVER,** FURTHERMORE.

_____

_____

_____

_____

_____

_____

_____

_____

_____

_____

Draw one or more images, in 30 seconds each. Choose images which will help you remember the main ideas.

Label each image with 6 key words.

Act V, *Scene* 3

Dunsinane. A room in the castle

[Enter MACBETH, Doctor, and Attendants]

Macbeth. Bring me no more reports; let them fly all:
Till Birnam wood remove to Dunsinane,
I cannot taint with fear. What's the boy Malcolm?
Was he not born of woman? The spirits that know
All mortal consequences have pronounced me thus: **2250**
'Fear not, Macbeth; no man that's born of woman
Shall e'er have **power** upon thee.' Then fly,
false thanes,
And mingle with the English epicures:
The mind I sway by and the heart I bear **2255**
Shall never sag with doubt nor shake with fear.
[Enter a Servant]
The devil damn thee black, thou cream-faced loon!
Where got'st thou that goose look?

Servant. There is ten thousand—**2260**

Macbeth. Geese, villain!

Servant. Soldiers, sir.

Macbeth. Go prick thy face, and over-red thy fear,
Thou lily-liver'd boy. What soldiers, patch?
Death of thy soul! those linen cheeks of thine **2265**
Are counsellors to fear. What soldiers, whey-face?

Servant. The English force, so please you.

Macbeth. Take thy face hence.
[Exit Servant]
Seyton!—I am sick at heart, **2270**
When I behold—Seyton, I say!—This push
Will cheer me ever, or disseat me now.
I have lived long enough: my way of life
Is fall'n into the sear, the yellow leaf;
And that which should accompany old age, **2275**
As honour, love, obedience, troops of friends,
I must not look to have; but, in their stead,
Curses, not loud but deep, mouth-honour, breath,
Which the poor heart would fain deny, and dare not. Seyton!

[Enter SEYTON]

Seyton. What is your gracious pleasure?

Macbeth. What news more?

Seyton. All is confirm'd, my lord, which was reported.

Macbeth. I'll fight till from my bones my flesh be hack'd.
Give me my armour.**2285**

Seyton. 'Tis not needed yet.

Macbeth. I'll put it on.
Send out more horses; skirr the country round;
Hang those that talk of fear. Give me mine armour.
How does your patient, doctor?**2290**

Doctor. Not so sick, my lord,
As she is troubled with thick coming fancies,
That keep her from her rest.

Macbeth. Cure her of that.
Canst thou not minister to a mind diseased, **2295**
Pluck from the memory a rooted sorrow,
Raze out the written troubles of the brain
And with some sweet oblivious antidote
Cleanse the stuff'd bosom of that perilous stuff
Which weighs upon the heart?**2300**

Doctor. Therein the patient
Must minister to himself.

Macbeth. Throw physic to the dogs; I'll none of it.
Come, put mine armour on; give me my staff.
Seyton, send out. Doctor, the thanes fly from me. **2305**
Come, sir, dispatch. If thou couldst, doctor, cast
The water of my land, find her disease,
And purge it to a sound and pristine health,
I would applaud thee to the very echo,
That should applaud again.—Pull't off, I say.— **2310**
What rhubarb, cyme, or what purgative drug,
Would scour these English hence? Hear'st thou of them?

Doctor. Ay, my good lord; your royal preparation
Makes us hear something.

Macbeth. Bring it after me. **2315**
I will not be afraid of death and bane,
Till Birnam forest come to Dunsinane.

Doctor. *[Aside]* Were I from Dunsinane away and clear,
Profit again should hardly draw me here.*[Exeunt]*

Key Question

Is Macbeth aware he is a tragic hero?

Grade 6

At this stage Macbeth has accepted the futility of his military position. He is surrounded. Many of the thanes and their soldiers have already left to join the English. And yet he knows the witches' prophecies are still true, he will still not be "vanquish'd" "till" Bihrnam Wood comes against him. He knows it will happen, but can't envisage how. He can't understand how the wood will "come against him" and he has no idea how "the **power** of man" can kill him if that man is not "of woman born".

Grade 7

But this is not the same as thinking he is invincible. He is not an idiot. He knows his end is coming and yet the manner of his death, his **fate**, is still a mystery.

Now he embraces **nihilism** and the accepts the approach of death. "I **have** lived **long** enough: **my way** of **life** / Is **fall'n** in**to** the **sear**". The **iambic stress** is on "have" and "long" as though he is answering a question about whether he has lived a long time. Yes, he seems to say, I have lived too long.

Grade 8

The **iambic** form is broken with a double **stress** on "my way", as though he accepts full responsibility for the decisions he has taken, certainly since becoming king. There is no hint of blaming others.

To **emphasise** this length of time he's lived, he chooses words with long vowel sounds, and forces the actor to linger on the **alliteration** of "lived long" to show that Macbeth is ready to welcome death. Compressing time in this way allows him to feel old, so that his life is "fall'n into the sear". "Fall" is also a deliberate **allusion** to the "fall" of Adam and Eve, so that **Shakespeare** reminds us of Macbeth's great sin.

He is in a hurry to end his life, but will not commit suicide. He still wishes to die in battle, true to himself. "I'll **fight** till **from** my **bones** my **flesh** be **hack'd**. / Give **me** my **arm**our." He seems to welcome this extremely violent and painful death, revealed by his violent **imagery**. **Ironic**ally, he is referred to by Malcolm at the end as a "butcher, whereas here his **semantic field** reminds us of a butcher. This is possibly a reflection of how he sees his own treatment of his victims. **Because** he has butchered others, he expects to be butchered himself. Even here we can see his great pride, refusing to surrender, or choose an easy death, which committing suicide would be.

Summarise this in one brilliant sentence.

_____

_____

_____

_____

_____

The **iambic** also **emphasises** this pride, so that the **stress** is not on "give" but "me". It's interesting that he **emphasises** his own pride and identity at the same time as he imagines losing that identity in death. His consolation is that he will die as a "soldier", the only **role** he fully inhabits. In performance, **however**, we can well imagine all the **syllables** are **stress** ed, "**Give me my armour**" in order to express his urgency, his eagerness to meet his death in battle.

In a play where Macbeth uses the **imagery** of clothing to define his feelings, we get the sense that he is throwing off the "borrowed robes" of kingship. When he puts on his "armour" he becomes his true self, a warrior, even though "Tis not needed yet."

Shakespeare interrupts this urgency to fight, with the arrival of the Doctor. The Doctor could easily have entered first, and news of the "ten thousand" English could have interrupted him. The **plot** and tension would have been the same. So, why does **Shakespeare** bring him on now? It is to give us a better understanding of Macbeth's love for his wife:

> "Cure her of that.
> Canst thou not minister to a mind diseased,
> Pluck from the memory a rooted sorrow."

He takes time out of the urgency of his preparations and the **nihilism** he feels about his own life, to look after Lady Macbeth. When he hopes the doctor could help her, he addresses the doctor **formally,** asking after "your patient". But once he receives a poor diagnosis, he reverts to "thou". Notice how he asks for a "cure" for her mental anguish and guilt, rather than for his own. The **metaphor** of "a rooted sorrow" does not apply to him, as though he himself does not feel "sorrow" for his crimes.

His feelings **therefore** are all for Lady Macbeth. He then asks the doctor an extraordinary, rhetorical question:

> "If thou couldst, doctor, cast
> The water of my land, find her disease,
> And purge it to a sound and pristine health."

This double **reference** to "disease" must be deliberate. He is implying that Scotland and Lady Macbeth have both been infected, made ill. Now, from the **audience**'s **perspective**, the infection is Macbeth. His act of *regicide* and continued slaughter has infected the country of Scotland. **Shakespeare** also **contrasts** this with the **image** he gave Malcolm, describing the English king's healing touch.

But Macbeth is asking a deeper question. What is it which has caused repeated war, repeated betrayal and women desperate for **power** and control? What is that disease? This is a **social** question. The answer is the **martial** nature of this **patriarchal society**, which is addicted to violence and **social status**, and determined to treat women as **inferior**. It is as though Macbeth wants a **society** which does not breed soldiers like him, and does not exclude women from influence, like his wife and the weird sisters. It is a moment when he stands apart from his own **fate** and asks what is wrong with **society**, and then asks for a cure.

Build Long Term Memory!

Draw an image in 30 seconds which will help you remember the main ideas.

Label it with 6 key words.

Write 3 sentences. The first words of each one must be in this order. **BECAUSE**, BUT, SO.

_____

_____

_____

_____

_____

_____

_____

_____

_____

Write 3 sentences. Use the words highlighted in the notes (as these are subject terminology).

_____

_____

_____

_____

_____

_____

Dunsinane. Within the castle

[Enter MACBETH, SEYTON, and Soldiers, with drum and colours]

Macbeth. Hang out our banners on the outward walls;
The cry is still 'They come:' our castle's strength
Will laugh a siege to scorn: here let them lie **2355**
Till famine and the ague eat them up:
Were they not forced with those that should be ours,
We might have met them dareful, beard to beard,
And beat them backward home.
[A cry of women within] **2360**
What is that noise?

Seyton. It is the cry of women, my good lord.

[Exit]

Macbeth. I have almost forgot the taste of fears;
The time has been, my senses would have cool'd **2365**
To hear a night-shriek; and my fell of hair
Would at a dismal treatise rouse and stir
As life were in't: I have supp'd full with horrors;
Direness, familiar to my slaughterous thoughts
Cannot once start me. **2370**
[Re-enter SEYTON]
Wherefore was that cry?

Seyton. The queen, my lord, is dead. (6 **syllables**)

Macbeth. She should have died hereafter; (7 **syllables**)
There would have been a time for such a word. **2375**
To-morrow, and to-morrow, and to-morrow,
Creeps in this petty pace from day to day
To the last **syllable** of recorded time,
And all our yesterdays have lighted fools
The way to dusty death. Out, out, brief candle! **2380** (11 **syllables**)
Life's but a walking shadow, a poor player (11 **syllables**)
That struts and frets his hour upon the stage
And then is heard no more: it is a tale
Told by an idiot, full of sound and fury, (11 **syllables**)
Signifying nothing. **2385** (6 **syllables**)
[Enter a Messenger]
Thou comest to use thy tongue; thy story quickly.

Messenger. Gracious my lord,
I should report that which I say I saw,
But know not how to do it.**2390**

Macbeth. Well, say, sir.

Messenger. As I did stand my watch upon the hill,
I look'd toward Birnam, and anon, methought,
The wood began to move.

Macbeth. Liar and slave!**2395**

Messenger. Let me endure your wrath, if't be not so:
Within this three mile may you see it coming;
I say, a moving grove.

Macbeth. If thou speak'st false,
Upon the next tree shalt thou hang alive, **2400**
Till famine cling thee: if thy speech be sooth,
I care not if thou dost for me as much.
I pull in resolution, and begin
To doubt the *equivocation* of the fiend
That lies like truth: 'Fear not, till Birnam wood **2405**
Do come to Dunsinane:' and now a wood
Comes toward Dunsinane. Arm, arm, and out!
If this which he avouches does appear,
There is nor flying hence nor tarrying here.
I gin to be aweary of the sun, **2410**
And wish the estate o' the world were now undone.
Ring the alarum-bell! Blow, wind! come, wrack!
At least we'll die with harness on our back.

[Exeunt]

Key Question

What effect does Lady Macbeth's suicide have on Macbeth?

Grade 6

Macbeth reacts with a hint of fear at the "cry of women". He probably suspects it is news he has dreaded, the death of Lady Macbeth: "I have almost forgot the taste of fears; / The time has been, my senses would have cool'd".

The conventional **view** is that Lady Macbeth dies off stage so that **Shakespeare** can show the distance between her and Macbeth. This is not a love story. After all, Juliet dies on stage, next to her Romeo. **Shakespeare contrasts** with that, so Macbeth doesn't even go to find her body. He doesn't allow himself any grief, simply complaining that she has chosen a very bad time to commit suicide. So he observes, "She should have died hereafter", meaning at a more convenient time.

Instead, he is more wrapped up in his own feelings: "I gin to be aweary of the sun" and decides that his life has been pointless, "**signify**ing nothing". He gives lady Macbeth barely a second thought to reflect that she now signifies "nothing" to him either.

Grade 7

Obviously, I am going to argue that this does not fit at all with the same Macbeth who moments ago stopped all thoughts of battle to get Lady Macbeth medical help for her sleepwalking and guilt.

But his stronger emotion is nostalgia: I have almost forgot the taste of fears;
The time has been, my senses would have cool'd". He is looking forward to feeling a sense of fear again, as though he has become numb through his bloodthirsty slaughter. A sense of yearning is created with the real sense of "taste", as though he wants to savour fear again. It explains his **nihilism, because** he now finds it almost impossible to feel normal emotions. But perhaps it also explains his attraction to battle. Only on the battle field can he hope to experience true fear.

When he hears of Lady Macbeth's death, he appears to react unemotionally, "She should have died hereafter". Many critics see this as indifference, and proof that he is simply preoccupied with himself, and out of love with his wife.

Grade 8

But we have already seen that he is looking forward to his own death, and desperate to find a "cure" for his wife's "diseased" mind. If we take his words literally, he means that he had hoped she would live, that the doctor would have helped her. We can also **infer** a level of upset from the seven **syllable** line, and his failure to use **pentameter**.

In addition, the **language** he uses to remember Lady Macbeth suggests his love for her. His **metaphor** likens her to a "brief candle," to lament that her life was too short. But a candle also **symbolises** light, as though her death now leaves him in darkness. This again suggests a **powerful** love for her.

Grade 9

In "Out, out, brief candle!" **Shakespeare** gives Macbeth a direct quotation from his wife, "Out, out". He deliberately changes her "damned spot" to the much more positive "candle", a deliberate **contrast** from darkness of hell to light.

On the one hand, this reflects his unnatural **perspective**, suggesting Macbeth is worshipping evil. This allows a *Jacobean* **audience** to enjoy his final punishment as divine justice. On the other hand, it reflects the strong bond of love he has for Lady Macbeth. Her words have become a part of him, **because** he still loves her. His emotional upset at her death is also conveyed in how he loses control of the **pentameter** in these two lines, which both have eleven **syllables**.

Her death **therefore** causes him to reflect on the purpose of life.

Write 2 sentences. Use the words highlighted in the notes (as these are subject terminology).

_____

_____

_____

_____

_____

Shakespeare gives him very personal **imagery**, perhaps as close as we might get to **Shakespeare**'s **view** of the world. He makes Macbeth liken life to a bad actor:

> "Life's but a walking shadow, a poor player
> That struts and frets his hour upon the stage".

Life is disappointing **because** it is not enough. Life is dressed up as attractive, but is full of vanity, "it struts". And full of anxiety, it "frets". This is an interesting rejection of what **society** values, which is **status**. Here, Macbeth criticises his own and Lady Macbeth's pursuit of ultimate **status**, which led to *regicide*. But he also thinks this is typical of all "life", and **therefore** of all people. It is simply that **society** itself is like a bad actor, attracted to **status**, behaving ridiculously on stage in an effort to steal the limelight, and failing.

He also sees life as both brief, taking a **metaphorical** "hour", but also lived for the entertainment of an **audience**, as it takes place on "the stage". This implies the greater **audience** is either **society**, or God. It suggests that life is wasted on us. We either live it to satisfy **social** values others impose on us, or we live it in order to please a God who will finally judge us.

Although he has become king and achieved the highest possible **social status**, it has brought him no joy. A *Jacobean* **audience** would see this as a just punishment for *regicide*. But Macbeth is arguing that this punishment is actually universal. **Society** does not let us choose to be who we truly are, but makes us follow a series of rules, laws, customs and beliefs. A belief in hell stops us enjoying any behaviour that challenges these customs and beliefs. We are only bad actors **because** someone else, **society** or God, has written the script of our lives.

Summarise this in one brilliant sentence.

_____

_____

_____

Again, a *Jacobean* **audience** will see this as a part of his divine punishment. He has been the "idiot, full of sound and fury" who has pursued an empty ambition. Having become king, he has found his life is meaningless, "**signify**ing nothing" **because** everything he values will be taken from him: first his friendship with Banquo, next his relationship with his wife, next her life, then any hope for his own future, and finally any hope of legacy and an heir. By now you will also have spotted it is an 11 **syllable** line, which begins with a **trochee**. Normally this has indicated an evil intention or deceit. This time it might suggest that **society** is wrong.

However, Macbeth is making a universal point. All our lives are brief, and we live them out as though our "sound" matters, and as though the story of our lives has meaning. But actually, our stories do not make sense, which is why they are "told by an idiot."

An even more subversive idea for a *Jacobean* **audience** is his attack on God. In a **Christian society**, the "tale" or script of your life is told by God. Here he confronts God as an "idiot", and the stories of the Bible as nonsensical. The idea of living a **Christian** life **signifies** "nothing". This isn't atheism. Macbeth still has a belief in God. But he argues that if **fate** exists, then free will has been an illusion. He has just been following a script. He believes God's idea of free will is a lie.

Aristotle defined the **tragic hero** as having an **anagnorisis**, the moment when the **protagonist** comes to a profound realisation about himself, or a situation. We can certainly argue that this is when Macbeth **verb**alises his **anagnorisis**, so we can understand his **view** of his own **character** and life, and also the **nihilism** he feels about his own **society**.

Shakespeare stands outside this. He must want his **audience** to wonder about his own **viewpoint**, as he so obviously shows off with this theatrical **metaphor**. What, we ask, does **Shakespeare** think about this?

We can't know for sure. But it is interesting that he refuses to be the "poor player". **Shakespeare** is not reported to be a star of his plays, though he did act in some. We can **infer** that he instead writes the "tale". On the one hand, he is joking with his **audience**. The "idiot" who has written Macbeth's tale is actually **Shakespeare**, himself. But on the other hand, he has stepped outside **fate**, writing his own life's "tale".

Summarise this in one brilliant sentence.

_____

_____

_____

_____

Only a generation before **Shakespeare**, men were destined to follow in their father's footsteps. It was extremely rare to become independently wealthy. The quickest way to advancement (if you survived) was through the military, as Macbeth has done. But in **Shakespeare**'s London, a whole new entertainment industry had grown up. Each actor and each playwright invented themselves, from often humble origins. The idea that we are in charge of our own futures is a modern idea, created by a free education for all. In **Shakespeare**'s time it was a pretty revolutionary idea.

Shakespeare would look about him and see himself as a man who had successfully changed his destiny and written his own **fate**. Several of his fellow playwrights had been educated at Oxford and Cambridge universities, but **Shakespeare** was from a much poorer and less educated background.

Shakespeare's play is set nearly 600 years before his present. When he **portrays** Macbeth as a victim of **fate**. Shakespeare may be **contrasting** this with the opportunities he has taken. But for women, there has been no change in **social** opportunity in those 600 years. In this **soliloquy** Lady Macbeth, **however**, lives a life no different from _Jacobean_ women, which is part of **Shakespeare**'s political point.

Macbeth is not just talking about himself, **because** he is thinking of Lady Macbeth's death. He is referring to her as a "poor player", the victim of a **fate society** has written for her. Her **tragedy** is that **society** has given her a belief in God. This is accompanied by a belief in the soul, and in eternal damnation in hell.

Macbeth only mentions the idea of his soul going to hell once, "and mine eternal jewel / Given to the common enemy of man". But this is in a speech dominated by thoughts of Banquo's sons, which upsets him much more. He doesn't name the soul – it is an "eternal jewel" – and he doesn't name the devil, he is just "the common enemy of man". These suggest this is a rhetorical point of **view**. He doesn't really believe in hell. He may not even believe in the soul. He does believe in posterity and history, and challenges "**fate**" to try to change his history and posterity. **Because** he doesn't believe in hell, his final feelings in this *scene* are **nihilistic**:

> "I gin to be aweary of the sun,
> And wish the estate o' the world were now undone."

The "sun" is a **metaphor** for life, so he is now prepared for death. But "sun" is also **symbolic** of God and kingship. Here, Macbeth has tired of being king. He is also tired of the **Christian perspective** of the world. His second line, wanting to undo "the estate o'the world" suggests that he deliberately attacks God's creation, the world God has made. Again, this is not atheistic, as he still believes in God. Instead it is a blasphemous criticism of God himself. This makes the **audience** keen for his death, **because** Macbeth attacks their faith.

Interestingly, Macbeth is also making a political point. To a *Jacobean* **audience**, "estate" didn't just mean the 'state' of the world. It also referred to **status** and aristocracy. We can see that Macbeth means the political system which places the king at the top of the *Great Chain of Being*, and of the political order. He is arguing against kingship.

Again, this is a *heretical* idea, and would also confirm Macbeth's attack on God, and helps the *Jacobean* **audience** look forward to his oncoming death. From their **perspective**, this is another reason he deserves to be executed and his soul sent to hell. But it is possibly a hint from **Shakespeare** that **society** would be better with a different **social** hierarchy and "estate". It is possible that this is demonstrated by the lack of rights of women, **dramatised** by Lady Macbeth's despair and suicide.

Write 3 sentences. Use as many of these words as you can: BECAUSE, ALTHOUGH, THEREFORE, HOWEVER, FURTHERMORE.

_____

_____

_____

_____

_____

_____

_____

_____

_____

In order to overcome his sense of **nihilism**, he tries to meet his death with purpose. He chooses bloodlust once more, and is determined to die in battle: "At least we'll die with harness on our back." This is **characteristic** of a **tragic hero**, who knows that **fate** can't be escaped, but fights on anyway.

Build Long Term Memory!

> **Draw an image in 30 seconds which will help you remember the main ideas.**
>
>
>
>
>
>
>
>
>
>
>
>
>
>
> **Label it with 6 key words.**

> **Go back over this whole section and pick out the top 4 ideas you need to remember.**
>
> 1._____
>
> _____
>
> _____
>
> 2._____
>
> _____
>
> _____
>
> 3._____
>
> _____
>
> _____
>
> 4._____
>
> _____

Another part of the field.

[Enter MACBETH]

Macbeth. Why should I play the Roman fool, and die
On mine own sword? whiles I see lives, the gashes
Do better upon them.**2475**

[Enter MACDUFF]

Macduff. Turn, hell-hound, turn!

Macbeth. Of all men else I have avoided thee:
But get thee back; my soul is too much charged
With blood of thine already.**2480** (7 **syllables**)

Macduff. I have no words: (4 **syllables**)
My voice is in my sword: thou bloodier villain
Than terms can give thee out!

[They fight]

Macbeth. Thou losest labour: **2485**
As easy mayst thou the intrenchant air
With thy keen sword impress as make me bleed:
Let fall thy blade on vulnerable crests;
I bear a charmed life, which must not yield,
To one of woman born.**2490** (6 **syllables**)

Macduff. Despair thy charm; (4 **syllables**)
And let the angel whom thou still hast served
Tell thee, Macduff was from his mother's womb
Untimely ripp'd. (4 **syllables**)

Macbeth. Accursed be that tongue that tells me so, **2495**
For it hath cow'd my better part of man!
And be these juggling fiends no more believed,
That palter with us in a double sense;
That keep the word of promise to our ear,
And break it to our hope. I'll not fight with thee.**2500**

Macduff. Then yield thee, coward,
And live to be the show and gaze o' the time:
We'll have thee, as our rarer monsters are,
Painted on a pole, and underwrit,
'Here may you see the tyrant.'**2505** (8 **syllables**)

Macbeth. I will not yield, (5 **syllables**)
To kiss the ground before young Malcolm's feet,

And to be baited with the rabble's curse.
Though Birnam wood be come to Dunsinane,
And thou opposed, being of no woman born, **2510**
Yet I will try the last. Before my body
I throw my warlike shield. Lay on, Macduff,
And damn'd be him that first cries, 'Hold, enough!'
[Exeunt, fighting. Alarums]
[Retreat. Flourish. Enter, with drum and colours,] **2515**
MALCOLM, SIWARD, ROSS, the other thanes, and Soldiers]

Malcolm. I would the friends we miss were safe arrived.

Siward. Some must go off: and yet, by these I see,
So great a day as this is cheaply bought.

Malcolm. Macduff is missing, and your noble son.**2520**

Ross. Your son, my lord, has paid a soldier's debt:
He only lived but till he was a man;
The which no sooner had his prowess confirm'd
In the unshrinking station where he fought,
But like a man he died.**2525**

Siward. Then he is dead?

Ross. Ay, and brought off the field: your cause of sorrow
Must not be measured by his worth, for then
It hath no end.

Siward. Had he his hurts before?**2530**

Ross. Ay, on the front.

Siward. Why then, God's soldier be he!
Had I as many sons as I have hairs,
I would not wish them to a fairer death:
And so, his knell is knoll'd.**2535**

Malcolm. He's worth more sorrow,
And that I'll spend for him.

Siward. He's worth no more
They say he parted well, and paid his score:
And so, God be with him! Here comes newer comfort.**2540**

[Re-enter MACDUFF, with MACBETH's head]

Macduff. Hail, king! for so thou art: behold, where stands
The usurper's cursed head: the time is free:
I see thee compass'd with thy kingdom's pearl,
That speak my salutation in their minds; **2545**

Whose voices I desire aloud with mine:
Hail, King of Scotland!

All. Hail, King of Scotland!

[Flourish]

Malcolm. We shall not spend a large expense of time **2550**
Before we reckon with your several loves,
And make us even with you. My thanes and kinsmen,
Henceforth be earls, the first that ever Scotland
In such an honour named. What's more to do,
Which would be planted newly with the time, **2555**
As calling home our exiled friends abroad
That fled the snares of watchful tyranny;
Producing forth the cruel ministers
Of this dead butcher and his fiend-like queen,
Who, as 'tis thought, by self and violent hands **2560**
Took off her life; this, and what needful else
That calls upon us, by the grace of Grace,
We will perform in measure, time and place:
So, thanks to all at once and to each one,
Whom we invite to see us crown'd at Scone.**2565**

[Flourish. Exeunt]

Key Question

Why does Macbeth choose to die fighting Macduff?

Grade 6

At this final *scene*, Macbeth knows he will be defeated. He contemplates suicide, like a "Roman fool", but decides against taking control of his moment and manner of death. He doesn't want to cheat **fate**, but fight on and find out how he will be killed by a man not "of woman born". He is desperate to solve this riddle, just as *Oedipus did with the Sphinx.*

Grade 7

But a greater attraction for Macbeth, as always, is bloodlust: "whiles I see lives, the gashes / Do better upon them." He simply wants to enjoy killing others. He has also begun to savour "the taste of fears" and is actively searching for the man who can kill him.

Although this is his final opportunity to enjoy killing, he avoids fighting Macduff. Perhaps the death of Lady Macbeth has made him reflect on the pain Macduff has felt when Macbeth slaughtered his family. He tells Macduff, "my soul is too much charged / With blood of thine already." This note of regret is unusual in Macbeth, and suggests that accepting his own death has led to a kind of **catharsis**, and a desire to put things right.

Grade 8

This care for Macduff is a reminder of his immense care for Lady Macbeth at the beginning of the battle. **Shakespeare ironic**ally makes Macbeth behave as a good king, once he knows he will be defeated. He cares for others, even treating his enemy with respect. It is an **ironic** return of "the milk o' human kindness".

Macduff insists on fighting. **Shakespeare** gives us a strong clue that he is losing, and Macbeth takes pity on him again, "Thou losest labour". Once Macbeth is winning the fight, he pauses to tell Macduff he can't be beaten, **because** "I bear a charmed life, which must not yield, / To one of woman born."

This is a surprising **interpretation**. The witches told him that none "of woman born shall harm" him. He, **however**, is looking for the person who will end his life. He must "yield" to that man. It is important to understand this. This is the reason he refuses to fight Macduff when he finds out that he was "from his mother's womb / Untimely ripped". He does not believe that Macduff can kill him in battle, so he has to give in to him, and "yield".

What are the 3 main ideas you want to remember so far?

1._____

_____

2._____

_____

3._____

_____

Grade 9

He also yields in another way with the **pentameter**. His line ending "of woman born" is 6 **syllables** long, and Macduff's reply is 4 **syllables** long. This is the only exchange between them which fits the **pentameter**. It perhaps suggests he accepts his **fate**, and is no longer fighting it.

But Macduff accuses him of cowardice. **Shakespeare** has brought Macbeth full circle. Lady Macbeth had accused him of cowardice in order to prompt him to kill Duncan. Macbeth has changed though, and won't be provoked now. Despite this taunt, he is willing to be thought a coward, and still "yield" to Macduff.

However, Macduff refuses to accept this, and will only kill Macbeth in battle. What persuades Macbeth is the thought of living, and having "To kiss the ground before young Malcolm's feet." This tells us that it is **status** which motivates him. He is happy to be remembered as a "tyrant", rather than as submissive and **inferior** to Malcolm.

Beyond Grade 9

There is also a political point here. Scotland's kings, as you remember, did not inherit the throne from their fathers. Instead, the king chose his successor. In a **martial society**, Malcolm was a poor choice, and Macbeth the only logical choice. Macbeth's political point is that he should have been king, rather than "young Malcolm".

Shakespeare could also be making a political point, that a **society** which does not fight over its heirs is likely to be more stable. This is another way of asking the nobles at court to accept James as their king.

Another way of looking at this is that Macbeth chooses his **fate** as a **tragic hero**. If he yields, and lives, he will have beaten **fate**, and broken the weird sisters' prophecies. But then he would not be a **tragic hero**, simply an object of pity.

His final words are **ambiguous**:

> "Before my body
> I throw my warlike shield. Lay on, Macduff,
> And damn'd be him that first cries, 'Hold, enough!'"

"Before" has the meaning of 'in front'. He means to fight to win, defending himself, even though he knows he hopes he will be killed. He knows that his soul is already "damn'd", so his words are to Macduff, instructing him not to beg for mercy.

Another possibility is that Macbeth is reckless once again. The **verb** "throw" also suggests he discards the shield in front of him, deliberately making himself vulnerable to Macduff's strikes. Both **interpretation**s show his acceptance and welcoming of his own death.

What are the 3 main ideas you want to remember so far?

1._____

_____

2._____

_____

3._____

_____

Although Malcolm ends the play with a speech offering the hope of peace and unity, **Shakespeare** introduces a discordant note. He has created the **character** of Young Siward to be killed by Macbeth, before the fight with Duncan. At that point it serves to underline Macbeth's feelings of invincibility, or his skill as a warrior.

However, once Macbeth is killed, **Shakespeare** now introduces Siward's father. His reaction to his son's death is horrifying to a modern **audience**. **Shakespeare** also finds it horrifying. Old Siward doesn't mourn his son's death **because** he had his injuries on his front, and **therefore** died facing his enemy rather than fleeing. Malcolm rejects this glorification of warrior **culture**.

> "**Malcolm.** He's worth more sorrow,
> And that I'll spend for him.
>
> **Siward.** He's worth no more
> They say he parted well, and paid his score".

This suggests that Malcolm has learned to "feel it like a man", as Macduff taught him with the death of his family. Old Siward represents the past, which worships a **martial society**, a warrior cult. His unfeeling sacrifice of its own son's is a condemnation of that **society**. **Shakespeare therefore** pleads for a more **culture**d and less warlike king.

However, we all know that Malcolm will be succeeded by Fleance at some point. So **Shakespeare** hints at the possibility of future war, in a **society** which values the warrior above all. We are reminded of the **symbolism** of Banquo's words to Fleance, "hold, take my sword" when he passes on his "warlike" self to his son. Perhaps **Shakespeare** hopes that this **metaphorical** sword has not been passed down to King James, and that he won't need to enter into battle against any of the nobles at court.

Build Long Term Memory!

Draw an image in 30 seconds which will help you remember the main ideas.

Label it with 6 key words.

Write 3 sentences. Use the words highlighted in the notes (as these are subject terminology).

_____

_____

_____

_____

_____

_____

_____

_____

Write 3 sentences. The first words of each one must be in this order. **BECAUSE**, BUT, SO.

_____

_____

_____

_____

_____

_____

_____

_____

_____

Write 3 sentences. Use as many of these words as you can: **BECAUSE, ALTHOUGH, THEREFORE, HOWEVER,** FURTHERMORE.

_____

_____

_____

_____

_____

_____

_____

_____

_____

_____

_____

_____

_____

Revise Act 5

Use the next page to summarise what you have learned during Act 5. You might:

4. Draw a mind map, using the pictures you have already used in your notes.
5. Present your learning in columns, focusing on 5 key quotations.
6. Something you prefer.

Quote	Terminology	Beautiful sentence	Context	Shakespeare's purpose	Alternative interpretation	Link to other part of play

Summarise your notes on the character of Macbeth

Summarise your notes on the character of Lady Macbeth

Summarise your notes on the character of Banquo

Summarise your notes on the weird sisters

Summarise your notes on Shakespeare's Purposes

Summarise your notes on Love and Marriage, Meter and Metaphor

Make notes on the 10 quotations you will try to use, no matter what the essay question on Macbeth